BASIC BUSINESS MATHEMATICS:

A Life-Skills Approach

Richard P. Truchon

P 70   17/7/92

CRISP PUBLICATIONS, INC.
Los Altos, California

BASIC BUSINESS MATHEMATICS:
A Life-Skills Approach

Richard P. Truchon

CREDITS
Editor: **W. Philip Gerould & Tony Hicks**
Design and Composition: **Interface Studio**
Cover Design: **Carol Harris**

Copyright © 1990 by Crisp Publications, Inc.
Printed in the United States of America

Crisp books are distributed in Canada by Reid Publishing, Ltd., P.O. Box 7267, Oakville, Ontario, Canada L6J 6L6.

In Australia by Career Builders, P.O. Box 1051, Springwood, Brisbane, Queensland, Australia 4127.

And in New Zealand by Career Builders, P.O. Box 571, Manurewa, New Zealand.

Mathematics Study Skills, Pages 1-5
Adapted from Study Skills Strategies, Uelaine Lengefeld
Crisp Publications, 1988

Library of Congress Catalog Card Number 89-81953
Truchon, Richard P.
Basic Business Mathematics
ISBN 1-56052-024-8

To my wife
Lorraine

ACKNOWLEDGEMENTS

I thank my colleagues at New Hampshire Technical College, Professors Samuel Robinson and Eugene Rice for their suggestions and reviews of the manuscript. Thanks are also extended by my students who were assigned many of the exercises and this gave me the stimulus to continue writing.

Special thanks go to Ms. Brigitte Lussier for word processing the entire manuscript with incredible competence. I am most appreciative of the contributions made by Kathleen Barcos, Production Editor.

Finally, I wish to thank my wife, Lorraine for her continued support, patience, and faith during the writing of this book.

CONTENTS

PREFACE vii
STUDY SKILLS 1

PART I   BASICS

1.0 Whole Numbers 7
    1.1 Rounding Off 8
    1.2 Addition 11
    1.3 Subtraction 15
    1.4 Multiplication 19
    1.5 Division 23
2.0 Fractions 27
    2.1 Proper and Improper Fractions 27
    2.2 Addition of Like Fractions 33
    2.3 Lowest Common Denominator 33
    2.4 Addition of Unlike Fractions 35
    2.5 Subtraction of Fractions 37
    2.6 Multiplication of Fractions 39
    2.7 Division of Fractions 41
3.0 Decimals 45
    3.1 Converting Fractions to Decimals 45
    3.2 Converting Decimals to Fractions 47
    3.3 Adding Decimal Numbers 49
    3.4 Subtracting Decimal Numbers 51
    3.5 Rounding Off Decimal Numbers 53
    3.6 Multiplying Decimal Numbers 54
    3.7 Dividing Decimal Numbers 57
4.0 Percent 59

PART II   APPLICATIONS

5.0 Equations 65
6.0 Formulas 70
7.0 The Percentage Formula 74
    7.1 Solving Problems with the Percentage Formula 74
    7.2 Commissions 79
    7.3 Percent Increase (Mark-up) 83
    7.4 Percent Decrease (Mark-down) 87
    7.5 Discount 91
    7.6 Sales Tax 93
    7.7 Property Tax 97
    7.8 Simple Interest 101
    7.9 Installment Loans 107

CONTENTS

PART III   GRAPHS

8.0 Bar Graphs 115
9.0 Line Graphs 122
10.0 Circle Graphs 126

POST TEST 131

PREFACE

There is an emerging knowledge economy which is impacting our country's global leadership. Countries such as Japan and West Germany have a higher mathematics and science proficiency than the United States. On a more personal level, each of us must become more numerate if we wish to succeed in the ever-changing technological environment. Knowledge permeates every aspect of our lives, because our knowledge translates into highly skilled jobs, higher wages, and a better quality of life.

This book was written to help the reader improve his or her basic mathematics skills using a self-study approach. The book follows this structure: the introduction to each concept is followed by examples, exercises, and answers to the exercises. In doing the exercises, it is strongly recommended that the reader use a calculator. Calculators are commonly used throughout the business world.

The best way to learn mathematics is to solve problems! This book will enable you to improve your basic skills in a friendly, practical way. To paraphrase an ancient Chinese proverb: When I hear mathematics, I think about it; when I see mathematics, I remember it; when I do mathematics, I understand it.

This text uses mathematical knowledge and skills to solve problems that commonly occur in business and at home. We all encounter such life-skill problems as working with percentage, ratio, and proportion; paying sales tax; borrowing or investing money; being paid a commission; purchasing discounted products on sale; using credit cards; and so on. As educated people, we need to understand the mathematics used in these situations. We can't always rely on someone else to do our thinking for us.

When you have mastered the information in this text, you will be better prepared to use mathematics in your daily life.

MATHEMATICS STUDY SKILLS

Mathematics requires special study skill techniques. This brief section will provide a few tips and ideas which should make your math study skills more effective.

Because math can be confusing, it will sometimes be necessary to ask for special help. If you become confused or lost, seek the assistance of a tutor. Mathematics often builds on a set of rules, and if basic principles are not understood, the likelihood is that you will stay lost.

TIPS

| Tip 1 | Copy all the theorems, principles, and definitions *exactly*. Do not paraphrase or condense anything that is written on the board. *Also* be sure to copy the instuctor's explanation. Draw arrows to the instructor's explanation for each step of the problem. |

| Tip 2 | Rewrite math notes each day in ink for clarity and permanence. *Neatness* is especially important because of the need for accuracy. |

| Tip 3 | *Rework model problems* over and over until you can do them without stopping. This is the crucial step that most students overlook. Instead of figuring out what is being taught in the model problem, they jump right into doing homework, and end up reworking problems several times. |

| Tip 4 | Plan to work *at least two hours* on math homework for every hour of class time. Since you may need to spend ten to twelve hours working on math class assignments, set your priorities carefully and take a lighter academic load if possible. |

| Tip 5 | Learn the five R's of math shown on the next page. |

THE FIVE Rs OF MATH

RECOPY YOUR NOTES

REWORK THE MODEL

RECITE OUT LOUD

RECHECK YOUR WORK

TEST YOUR ANSWERS FOR
REASONABLENESS

PLAN OF ATTACK

To help you get an overview of the best math study skills, read the following 5 Rs for Math. Write recall cues to help you remember R1, R2, R3, R4, and R5.

THE 5 Rs OF MATH

RECALL CUES

R₁ **RECOPY** your notes in pen. Color-code definitions, rules, and problem areas. Neatness and legibility are your first step toward becoming a better math student.

> How do you rate your math notes?
> ☐ Organized and clear
> ☐ Messy
> ☐ Disorganized but neat

R₂ **REWORK** the model or example over and over until you can do it without hestitation.

> Have you ever taken this step before beginning the exercises?
> ☐ YES ☐ NO
> If not, try it and see if it makes a difference.

R₃ **RECITE.** Oral recitation is one more technique for improving your mathematical skills. Practice this step with a study partner or friend. Force each other to explain out loud each step of the process. If you are studying alone, you can still express your thinking aloud.

> Have you ever used this oral recitation technique when you were studying math?
> ☐ YES ☐ NO
> (Problem solving out loud is not a sign of senility but the mark of a critical thinker.)

4

RECALL
CUES

—————
————— R_4
—————

RECHECK your computations. Also recheck your thinking process. This is even more important when you move from one step of a problem to the next, or from one concept to a new one.

> ''MINDCHATTER''*
>
> When the internal thinking of professionals was questioned and recorded by Dr. Arthur Whimbey and Dr. Jack Lochhead, a typical dialogue was similar to the following:
>
> 1. ''Let me read the question again to be sure what's being asked. I'll circle or underline the question.''
>
> 2. ''Okay. I see, but I'll read it again to be sure.''
>
> 3. ''Slow down. Don't rush.''
>
> 4. ''What is given? What is known?''
>
> 5. ''How can I diagram, make a chart, or draw a visual to help me?''
>
> In all cases, lawyers, doctors, engineers, and other professionals were painstakingly careful to reread phrases and double-check their work.

—————
————— R_5
—————

Test for **REASONABLENESS.** Plug your answer into the problem to see if it makes sense. This final check could save you time and embarrassment later.

> Asking questions about how reasonable an answer is will make critical thinking a habit and a problem solving less ominous.

* Adapted from Arthur Whimbey and Jack Lochhead, *Problem Solving and Comprehension,* 4th ed., (Lawrence Erlbaum Associates, 1986).

PART

I

Basics

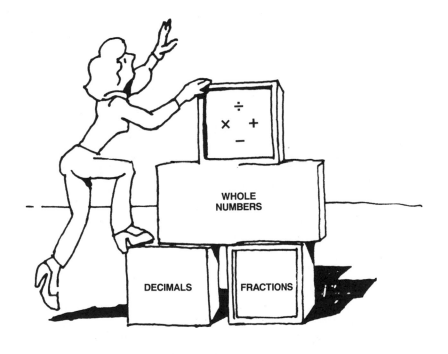

1.0 WHOLE NUMBERS

Most of us are familiar with two languages: a qualitative language (such as English or French) and a quantitative language (mathematics). In our qualitative language we use symbols (words) to represent concepts; for example, the word *dog* represents a dog. Similarly, in our quantitative language we use symbols (numbers) to represent number concepts; for example, *391* represents the number three hundred ninety-one. The arrangement of the symbols is important. The meaning of the concept will change if we write *god* instead of *dog*, or *193* in place of *391*. The letters of the alphabet are our written qualitative symbols; the digits of our number system are our quantitative symbols. In this text we will limit our discussion to the decimal or base-ten number system.

As children we learned about mathematics by counting with the *natural numbers*: 1, 2, 3, 4, 5, 6, 7, 8, 9. Later the number zero was introduced to give us a set of numbers known as the *whole numbers*. Each digit in a whole number has a place value. Moving from right to left increases the place value by a multiple of ten.

Example 1. Indicate the place values of the number 391.

3	9	1
Hundreds	Tens	Ones

"391" thus represents

$$
\begin{array}{rcr}
3 \times 100 & = & 300 \\
9 \times 10 & = & 90 \\
1 \times 1 & = & \underline{1} \\
& & 391
\end{array}
$$

or

$$300 + 90 + 1 = 391$$

This number is read as "three hundred ninety-one." *Note:* The word *and* is not used in reading whole numbers.

Example 2. What number does "42,113,786" represent?

4 2 , 1 1 3 , 7 8 6   represents

$$
\begin{array}{rcr}
4 \times 10,000,000 &=& 40,000,000 \\
2 \times 1,000,000 &=& 2,000,000 \\
1 \times 100,000 &=& 100,000 \\
1 \times 10,000 &=& 10,000 \\
3 \times 1,000 &=& 3,000 \\
7 \times 100 &=& 700 \\
8 \times 10 &=& 80 \\
6 \times 1 &=& 6 \\
\hline
&& 42,113,786
\end{array}
$$

$$40,000,000 + 2,000,000 + 100,000 + 10,000 + 3,000 + 700 + 80 + 6 = 42,113,786$$

This number is read as "forty-two million, one hundred thirteen thousand, seven hundred eighty-six."

1.1 Rounding Off Whole Numbers

When we say that a corporation's annual profit is $240,000, we are using an approximation. It may be that the actual profit is $239,781, but it is easier to use the number $240,000. The number has been *rounded off* to the nearest ten thousand. We rounded the number to $240,000 rather than $230,000 because $239,781 is closer to $240,000 than to $230,000. Here are some other examples of rounding off. 47 rounded to the nearest ten is 50; and 3,741 rounded to the nearest hundred is 3,700.

The procedure for rounding off whole numbers is:

1. Underline the digit in the place you are rounding to.

2. Look at the digit immediately to the right of the underlined digit. If the digit immediately to the right is greater than or equal to 5, add 1 to the underlined digit. If the digit immediately to the right is less than 5, don't change the underlined digit.

3. Replace all digits to the right of the underlined digit with zeros.

Example 1. Round 347 to the nearest hundred.

Step 1: Underline the hundreds digit: 357

Step 2: Look at the digit immediately to the right of the underlined digit. That digit is 5, so we increase 3 by 1: 457

Step 3: Replace all digits to the right of the underlined digit with zeros: 400.

Example 2. Round 350 to the nearest hundred.

350 ≈ 400

This is read as "three hundred fifty is approximately equal to four hundred."

Example 3. Round 341 to the nearest hundred.

341 ≈ 300

We will return to the concept of rounding off when we discuss decimals.

EXERCISE: 1.1

[handwritten:]
4 3 9 1
TH. HU. TEN O
N. ENS ES

4 × 1000   4000
3 × 100   300
9 × 10   91
1 × 00   1
———————
4391

1. Indicate the place value of each digit in the number 4,391.

2. Indicate the place value of the digit 7 in the number 8,473.   *7 × 10 = 70*   *8473 TENS*

3. Write eleven thousand, three hundred sixty-two in figures.   *11 362*

4. Write seven million, four hundred three in figures.   *7 000 403*

5. Write 345,678 in words.   *Three hundred forty-five thousand, six hundred seventy-eight*

6. Write 19,191 in words.   *Nineteen thousand, one hundred ninety-one*

7. Indicate the place value of each digit in the number 5,012.   *5 0 1 2   TH HU TEN O / N. ENS ES*

8. Name the place value of 7 in the number 173,245.   *7 TEN THOUSANDS*

9. Write one hundred seventeen thousand, three hundred forty-seven in figures.   *117 347*

10. Write 1,234 in words.   *One thousand, two hundred thirty four*

11. Write 403,057 in words.   *Four hundred three thousand, fifty seven*

12. Round 3,948 to the nearest ten.   *3950*

13. Round 3,948 to the nearest hundred.   *3900*

14. Round 3,948 to the nearest thousand.   *4000*

15. Round 169,750 to the nearest hundred thousand.   *200 000*

16. Round 7,500 to the nearest thousand.   *10 000*

17. Round 647 to the nearest hundred.   *600*

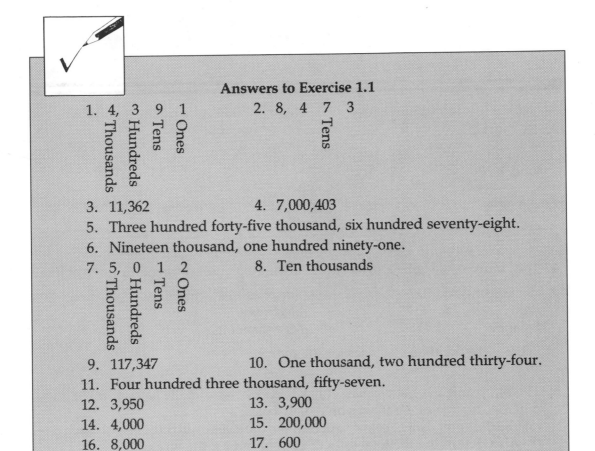

Answers to Exercise 1.1

1. 4, 3 9 1
   Thousands / Hundreds / Tens / Ones

2. 8, 4 7 3
   Tens

3. 11,362

4. 7,000,403

5. Three hundred forty-five thousand, six hundred seventy-eight.

6. Nineteen thousand, one hundred ninety-one.

7. 5, 0 1 2
   Thousands / Hundreds / Tens / Ones

8. Ten thousands

9. 117,347

10. One thousand, two hundred thirty-four.

11. Four hundred three thousand, fifty-seven.

12. 3,950

13. 3,900

14. 4,000

15. 200,000

16. 8,000

17. 600

1.2 Addition of Whole Numbers

The most frequently used operation is addition. The numbers being added are called *addends* and the result of the operation is called the *sum*.

Example 1. Add 2 + 11 + 3.

2 + 11 + 3 = 16
  addends   sum

Example 2. Add 341 + 24 + 19.

341
 24   addends
 19
───
384   sum

Since most businesses use computers today, you will find both the vertical and horizontal forms of addition when you use an electronic spreadsheet or other software.

Example 3. Use a calculator to add 68 + 47 + 2051.
The calculator sequence is:

on [68] [+] [47] [+] [2051] [=] 2166

EXERCISE 1.2

1. Add: 72
          33
          15

120

2. Add: 407
          939
          241
          102

1689

3. Add: 43 + 21 + 67.

131

4. The Pennyroyal Herb Farm had the following expenses during the month of June.

Advertising	$ 217	Supplies	$54
Rent	$ 934	Electricity	$98
Salaries	$3,478	Miscellaneous	$39

217 -
934 -
3478 -
54 -
98 -
39 -
4820

   What were the total expenses for the month?

5. The Shop and Save supermarket has been monitoring the sales of three different brands of cornflakes on a daily basis.
   (a) Use the spreadsheet below to determine the sales of all three brands each day.
   (b) Also determine the total sales of each brand for the week.
   (c) What were the total sales of all brands for the week?

	MON	TUES	WED	THURS	FRI	SAT	TOTAL
Brand K	4	10	7	11	15	5	*52*
Brand P	15	6	14	8	22	11	*76*
Brand G	7	13	9	9	10	9	*57*
	26	*29*	*30*	*28*	*47*	*25*	*185*

6. Add: 27
          57
          32
          19

135

7. Add: 1,307
          422
          196
          18
          3,002

4945

8. Add: 101 + 1,432 + 78 + 225. *1836*

9. Add: 1,492 + 203 + 1,938 + 64 + 373. *4070*

10. Charles had a balance of $713 in his checking account. He made the following deposits: $35, $118, $59, and $142. What is his new balance? *1067*

23,450
39,975
32,288
95,713

11. The attendance at a weekend rock concert was 23,450 on Saturday afternoon, 39,975 on Saturday evening and 32,288 on Sunday evening. What was the total attendance for the three performances?

12. As a salesperson you receive the following commissions: $467, $333, $570, $595, and $603. Find your total income from these commissions.

2568

13. Your biweekly paycheck shows the following deductions: FICA, $76; Federal income tax, $85; Retirement fund, $51; Health insurance, $7; Union dues, $3. What is the total amount of your deductions?

222

14. Use the spreadsheet below to determine (a) the commissions paid to all four salespersons each month, (b) the third-quarter commission for each salesperson, and (c) the total of commissions paid for the quarter.

Salesperson	July	August	September	Third-Quarter Commissions	
Maria	$1,385	$ 1,300	$ 793	*3478*	*830*
Joe	$ 781	$ 3,750	$11,028	*15559*	*123*
Mohammed	$9,830	$10,123	$ 899	*20852*	*899*
Yoko	$1,010	$ 903	$10,452	*12365*	*1852*
	13006	*16076*	*23172*	*52254*	*19 20852*
				52254	

15. Brigitte ordered three items from a mail order company. The three items weighed 2 lb 7 oz, 4 lb 8 oz, and 3 lb 9 oz. What was the total weight of the three items? (1 lb = 16 oz)

2 lb 7
4 lb 8
3 lb 9
10 lb 8 oz
24/16

14

Answers to Exercise 1.2

1. 120

2. 1,689

3. 131

4. $4,820

5. (a) Mon.: 26; Tues.: 29; Wed.: 30; Thurs.: 28; Fri.: 47; Sat.: 25;
   (b) Brand K: 52; Brand P: 76; Brand G: 57;
   (c) Total for the week: 185.

6. 135   7. 4,945

8. 1,836   9. 4,070

10. $1,067   11. 95,713

12. $2,568   13. $222

14. (a) July: $13,006; August: $16,076; September: $23,172;
    (b) Maria: $3,478; Joe: $15,559; Mohammed: $20,852; Yoko: $12,365;
    (c) Total third-quarter commissions: $52,254.

15. 10 lb 8 oz, or 10½ lb.

1.3 Subtraction of Whole Numbers

Subtraction is the operation of taking one number from another. The larger of the two numbers is called the *minuend*. The number being subtracted is called the *subtrahend*. The result of the subtraction is called the *difference*.

Example 1. Subtract 739 − 251.

$$
\begin{array}{rl}
739 & \text{minuend} \\
-\;251 & \text{subtrahend} \\
\hline
488 & \text{difference}
\end{array}
$$

Example 2. Subtract $3 from $10.

$10	−	$3	=	$7
minuend		subtrahend		difference

Subtraction is related to addition. In a sense, subtraction is another way of looking at the operation of addition. For any two whole numbers M and S, if $M − S = D$, then $D + S = M$.

Example 3. Consider the subtraction in Example 1.

739 − 251 = 488

What number must be added to 251 to give a sum of 739? The answer is 488.

251 + 488 = 739

If we want to subtract a larger number from a smaller number, we need a knowledge of algebra. We have to use *negative numbers*. For example, if the balance in our checking account is $47 and we write a check for $53, we have a deficit of $6. The balance of our account is − $6. In this book we will concentrate on subtraction problems where M is bigger than S.

Example 4. Stephen has $597 in his checking account. If he writes a check for $103, how much money will be left in his account?

$597 − $103 = 494

Example 5. Use a calculator to subtract 234 from 1007.

| 1007 | | − | | 234 | | = | 773 |

Example 6. Allan telephoned Dick and spoke for 9 minutes and 25 seconds. Later that day, Allan called Dick again and spoke for 5 minutes and 33 seconds. How much longer was the first call than the second?

      9 min 25 sec
  − 5 min 33 sec

We cannot subtract 33 seconds from 25 seconds, so we borrow 1 minute (60 seconds) from 9 minutes and convert 9 min 25 sec to 8 min 85 sec.

Thus our problem becomes:

      8 min 85 sec
  − 5 min 33 sec
      3 min 52 sec

The first call was 3 minutes and 52 seconds longer than the second.

EXERCISE 1.3

1. Subtract 309 from 1103.   *794*

2. Subtract 7801 − 46.   *7755*

3. Mary's pet cat weighs 9 lb 5 oz and Jane's pet cat weighs 6 lb 7 oz. How much more does Mary's cat weigh then Jane's? (1 lb = 16 oz)

   9 lb 5 / 6 7
   8 21 / 6 7 / 2 14

4. Kate jogged for 37 min 23 sec and Phil jogged for 23 min and 43 sec. (a) How much longer did Kate jog than Phil? (b) What was the combined jogging time for the two? (1 min = 60 sec)

   37 23   36 83 / 23 43   23 43 / (a) 13 40 / (b) 61 06 / (or) 1 1.06

5. The price of a used car is $4,300. During a sale week the price was reduced by $875. What was the new selling price?   *3425*

6.   495
   − 83   *+12*

7.   4,675
   − 2,503   *2672*

8. Subtract 12,948 − 3,631.   *9317*

9. 129,497 − 11,384 = ?   *118 113*

10. John has had $3,781 withheld from his wages this year. If he owes $2,973 in income taxes for the year, how much of a refund will he receive?   *$ 808*

11. Find the difference between eleven hundred fifty-nine and three thousand, four hundred twelve.   *2253*

12. Sandra bought a ski rack and optional locks for her car at a cost of $376. If the locks cost $35, what was the cost of the rack alone?   *$ 341*

13. Owner's equity is defined as the total assets minus the total liabilities. The August balance sheet for the Pennyroyal Tree Farm listed total assets at $247,934 and total liabilities at $213,529. Find the owner's equity.   *$ 34 405*

14. Sam recently purchased a computer for $2,375 and wrote a check for $850 as a down payment. Find the amount that remains to be paid.   *$1525*

15. A real estate agent rented 23 apartments in April, 31 apartments in May, and 47 apartments in June. How many more apartments must be rented in July if the agent's four-month quota is 130 apartments?   *29*

18

Answers to Exercise 1.3

1. 794

2. 7,755

3. 2 lb 14 oz

4. (a) 13 min 40 sec; (b) 1 hr 1 min 6 sec

5. $3,425

6. 412

7. 2,172

8. 9,317

9. 118,113

10. $808

11. 2,253

12. $341

13. $34,405

14. $1,525

15. 29 apartments

1.4 Multiplication of Whole Numbers

Multiplication is repeated addition of the same numbers. For example, 7×3 means $7 + 7 + 7$.

$$7 \times 3 = 7 + 7 + 7 = 21$$

The number that is multiplied is called the *multiplicand*. The number we multiply by is called the *multiplier*. The result of the multiplication is called the *product*. The multiplicand and multiplier are also called *factors*.

When we multiply two numbers that have more than one digit, we multiply each digit of the multiplicand by each digit of the multiplier to obtain a partial product. The sum of all of the partial products is the product.

Example 1. Multiply 218×37.

```
   218        multiplicand
 × 37         multiplier
 1526
  654         partial products
 8066         product
```

Example 2. Use a calculator to multiply 218×37.

| ON | 218 | × | 37 | = | *8066*

Example 3. If a gallon of paint costs $13 per gallon, how much would 27 gallons of paint cost?

$$\$13 \times 27 = \$351$$

EXERCISE 1.4

1. Multiply 791 × 103.   *81 473*

2. What is the cost of 15 VCRs if one VCR costs $325?   *$ 4 895*

3. A case of canned peas contains 24 cans. How many cans of peas would there be in 225 cases?   *5400*

4. Michele bought 7 concert tickets for $21 each and 3 more tickets for $15 each. What was her total bill?   *147*
   45
   $ 192

5. If your monthly salary is $1,260 and you can expect a yearly raise of $126 per month, what would be your earnings over a three-year period?   *15 120*
   16 632
   18 144
   49 896

6.   756   *2268*   7.   412 × 307 = ?
   × 23 *or 1512*
   17 348   17 388   *126 484*

8. A company orders 170 boxes of letterhead envelopes. If each box cost $23, find the total cost.   *$ 3910*

9. The division of community education at Calmina University charges tuition at a rate of $21 per credit. If a student has 15 credits during the fall semester, how much tuition will he pay?   *$ 315*

10. Elizabeth is the buyer for a Boston department store. She purchased 19 cases of men's socks, containing 40 pairs of socks in each case. If the socks cost $3 a pair, what is the total cost of the purchase?   *$ 2280*

11. You drive for 5 hours at a speed of 55 miles per hour. How many miles did you travel?   *$ 275 m*

12. Bob Hanson has a small apple orchard on his property. If each tree produces approximately 3 bushels of apples per season, how many bushels can he harvest from his orchard of 21 trees in one season?

63

13. It costs $31 a day, without mileage, to rent a car. How much does it cost to rent a car for 16 days, excluding mileage?

$ 496

14. The Ajax Company decided to install a phone in each of its employees' offices. If the company purchased 115 phones for $42 each, what was the total cost?

$ 4830

15. Skyway Airlines has 8 flights from Boston to Hartford each day. How many passengers per day can Skyway Airlines transport from Boston to Hartford if each flight can carry 175 passengers?

$ 1400

Answers to Exercise 1.4

1. 81,473

2. $4,875

3. 5,400

4. $192

5. $49,896

6. 17,388

7. 126,484

8. $3,910

9. $315

10. $2,280

11. 275 miles

12. 63 bushels

13. $496

14. $4,830

15. 1,400 passengers

1.5 Division of Whole Numbers

Division is finding how many times one number is contained in another. The number being divided is called the *dividend*. The number by which we are dividing is called the *divisor*. The result is called the *quotient*. If the divisor is not a multiple of the dividend, the remaining number is called a *remainder*.

Example 1. Divide 1,138 by 11

$$
\begin{array}{r}
103 \\
11\overline{)1138} \\
-11 \\
\hline
38 \\
-33 \\
\hline
5
\end{array}
$$

divisor   quotient   dividend   remainder

Just as multiplication can be thought of as repeated addition, so division can be thought of as repeated subtraction.

Example 2. Divide 35 by 5. Keep subtracting 5s from 35 until you're left with zero. The number of times that 5 is subtracted from 35 is the quotient. The quotient is 7 in this example.

	Number of subtractions		Number of subtractions
35		15	
− 5	1	− 5	5
30		10	
− 5	2	− 5	6
25		5	
− 5	3	− 5	7
20		0	
− 5	4		

Multiplication and division are related operations. We can use mutliplication to check our division. The divisor multiplied by the quotient will give the dividend, if there is a remainder of zero.

Example 3. Divide 35 ÷ 5 and check the answer.

$$5\overline{)35} \quad \overset{7}{}$$

Check: 7 × 5 = 35   The division is correct.

Note: The result of dividing by zero is undefined! You cannot divide by zero. Thus 14 ÷ 0 has no answer.

Example 4. Use your calculator to try 14 ÷ 0.

| 14 | | ÷ | | 0 | | = | *ERROR*

Occasionally students will forget that you can't divide by zero when they encounter 0 ÷ 0. Perhaps that error occurs because "any number divided by itself is one" is an often heard statement. The statement is incomplete, however; it should be, "any number *except zero...*"

Note that you can divide any number, except zero, into zero.

Example 5. Divide 0 ÷ 7.

$0 \div 7 = 0$

Example 6. Use a calculator to divide 10,215 by 15.

| ON | | 10215 | | ÷ | | 15 | | = | *681*

Example 7. If a car can travel for 810 miles on 45 gallons of gasoline, how far can it travel on 1 gallon of gasoline?

$$\begin{array}{r} 18 \\ 45\overline{)810} \end{array}$$ It can travel 18 miles on 1 gallon of gas.

The *average* of a set of numbers is defined as the sum of the numbers divided by the number of numbers. To find the average of a set of numbers, add them, and then divide by the number of addends.

Example 8. Carla made the following deposits in her checking account: $640, $830, $1056, and $700. What was Carla's average deposit?

Step 1: Add the amounts of the deposits.

$$\begin{array}{r} \$640 \\ 830 \\ 1,056 \\ \underline{700} \\ \$3,226 \end{array}$$

Step 2: Divide the total amount deposited ($3,226) by the number of deposits (4).

$$\begin{array}{r} \$806.50 \\ 4\overline{)3226.00} \\ \underline{32} \\ 26 \\ \underline{24} \\ 20 \\ \underline{20} \\ 0 \end{array}$$

Example 9. The following daily temperatures were recorded during the first week in January: S, 13°; M, 32°; T, 27°; W, 14°; Th, 29°; F, 0°; S, 5°. Find the average temperature for the week, to the nearest 0.1° using a calculator.

| 13 | | + | | 32 | | + | | 27 | | + | | 14 | | + | | 29 | | + | | 0 |

| + | | 5 | | = | | ÷ | | 7 | | = | 17.1°   The average temperature if 17.1°.

EXERCISE 1.5

1. Divide 960 by 16.   *60*

2. 0)0̄   *0 indefinite*

3. On an English exam, six students' scores were 76, 83, 68, 90, 92, and 95.
   What was their average score?   *84*

4. The total cost for lunch was $45, which included tax and gratuities. If four
   people agreed to divide the cost equally, what did each person pay?   *$ 11.25*

5. A business ordered 800 personal computers (PCs) at a total cost of $760,000.   *$ 950*
   Another order at the same price per PC came to $251,750. How many PCs
   were received on the second order?   *265*

6. (a) 624 ÷ 4   *156*   (b) 63,525 ÷ 75   *847*

7. Find the quotient of forty-one thousand, one hundred forty divided by
   sixty-eight.   *605.07*

8. The total cost of producing 475 calculators was $12,825. What is the unit cost
   (that is, the cost of producing 1 calculator)?   *$ 27*

9. Joey is expected to make an average of 7 sales calls per day. Last week she
   made 6 calls on Monday, 9 calls on Tuesday, 11 calls on Wednesday, 5 calls
   on Thursday and 10 calls on Friday. What was Joey's average? Did she meet
   her quota?   *8.2   yes*

10. A manufacturer produced 1,562 pairs of binoculars at a production cost of
    $23,430. What was the cost to produce one pair of binoculars?   *$ 15*

11. A state lottery prize of $4,832,125 was equally shared by 43 ticket holders.
    How much did each ticket holder receive?   *$ 112375*

12. How much do you earn per week if your annual salary is $40,716?   *$783*

13. ABC company's monthly wages are: manager, $1,320; accountant, $1,175;
    12 salespeople, $790 each, two bookkeepers, $630 each; custodian, $510.   *4265*
    What is the average monthly wage of an ABC company employee?   *9480*   *13765*
    $ 808.52

14. On a math exam, two students scored 95, five students scored 87, three
    students scored 73, four students scored 63, and one student scored 40.
    What was the class average?   *190*   *435*
    219   *252*   *40*   *1136 / 15*   *75.73*   *75.73   76%*

26

Answers to Exercise 1.5

1. 60

2. There is no quotient. You can't divide by zero.

3. $\frac{504}{6} = 84$

4. $4\overline{)\$45}$ $\$11.25$

5. $800\overline{)\$760,000}$ $\$950$ $950\overline{)251,750}$ 265 265 PCs

6. (a) 156;　　(b) 847

7. 605

8. $27

9. 8.2 calls per day; yes

10. $15

11. $112,375

12. $783

13. $808.53

14. 75.7 rounded to 76

2.0 FRACTIONS

Many business mathematics problems cannot be solved by using only whole numbers. We need to learn about fractions and their applications. A fraction is one number, the *numerator*, divided by another number, the *denominator*.

Example 1. Write ''three-fourths'' as a fraction.

$\dfrac{3}{4}$ numerator
denominator

The numerator is the number of equal parts being considered. The denominator is the number of equal parts that the whole has been divided into. The fraction $\frac{3}{4}$ can be represented as in Figure 2.1

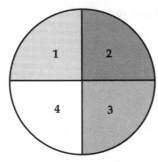

Figure 2.1   Three-fourths ($\frac{3}{4}$)

Recall that the only whole number which cannot be a denominator is zero. *Division by zero is impossible!* It is possible, however, to divide any whole number, except zero, into zero.

Example 2. What is the value of $\dfrac{7}{0}$?

$\frac{7}{0}$ does not exist. There's no number that can be multiplied by zero to give 7. Any number multiplied by zero gives a product of zero—never 7!

2.1   Proper and Improper Fractions

A *proper fraction* has a numerator which is less than its denominator, such as $\frac{3}{7}$. A proper fraction is smaller than 1. An *improper fraction* has a numerator which is greater than its denominator, such as $\frac{4}{3}$. An improper fraction is greater than 1.

Like fractions are fractions whose denominators are the same. For example, $\frac{1}{7}, \frac{3}{7}$, and $\frac{5}{7}$ are like fractions.

Unlike fractions are fractions whose denominators are different. For example, $\frac{1}{4}$, $\frac{2}{7}, \frac{5}{8}$, and $\frac{7}{11}$ are unlike fractions.

The fractions $\frac{5}{10}, \frac{6}{12}, \frac{7}{14}$, and $\frac{25}{50}$ could all be written as $\frac{1}{2}$. We say that $\frac{5}{10}$ is *reduced* or *simplified* to $\frac{1}{2}$, and that $\frac{5}{10}$ and $\frac{1}{2}$ are *equivalent fractions*. In any problem involving fractions it is usually helpful to reduce a fraction to its lowest terms before beginning your work. A fraction is reduced to its lowest terms if it can't be reduced any further, that is, if the only common factor of the numerator and denominator is 1.

Example 3. Reduce $\dfrac{2}{4}$ to its lowest terms.

$$\frac{2}{4} = \frac{1}{2} \qquad \text{See Figure 2.2.}$$

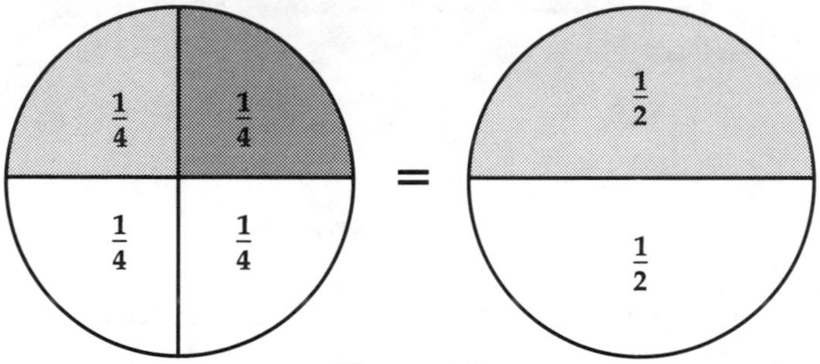

Figure 2.2

Example 4. Reduce $\dfrac{3}{12}$ to its lowest terms.

$$\frac{3}{12} = \frac{3 \times 1}{3 \times 4} = \frac{3}{3} \times \frac{1}{4} = 1 \times \frac{1}{4} = \frac{1}{4}$$

Example 5. Reduce $\dfrac{21}{56}$ to its lowest terms.

$$\frac{21}{56} = \frac{7 \times 3}{7 \times 8} = \frac{7}{7} \times \frac{3}{8} = 1 \times \frac{3}{8} = \frac{3}{8}$$

Here's a way to check whether two fractions are equivalent. Multiply the numerator of the first fraction by the denominator of the second fraction. Then multiply the numerator of the second fraction by the denominator of the first fraction. If the two products are equal, the fractions are equivalent.

Example 6. Are $\frac{3}{7}$ and $\frac{18}{42}$ equivalent?

$$\frac{3}{7} = \frac{18}{42} \qquad \text{They are equivalent.}$$

Therefore $3 \times 42 = 126$
$\qquad\quad 7 \times 18 = 126$

A *mixed number* consists of a whole number and a fraction, such as $2\frac{1}{3}$, read as ''two and one-third.'' It is permissible to use the word *and* here. $2\frac{1}{3}$ means 2 and $\frac{1}{3}$ or 2 plus $\frac{1}{3}$.

If we need to convert an improper fraction to a mixed number, we must divide the numerator by the denominator. The quotient is our whole number, and the remainder is the numerator of the fraction.

Example 7. Convert $\frac{5}{3}$ to a mixed number.

$$
\begin{array}{r}
1 \leftarrow \text{whole number} \\
3\overline{)5} \\
\underline{3} \\
2 \leftarrow \text{remainder}
\end{array}
$$

Therefore $\frac{5}{3} = 1\frac{2}{3}$

Conversely, if we wish to convert a mixed number to an improper fraction, we multiply the whole number by the denominator and add the numerator. This gives the new numerator; the denominator remains the same.

Example 8. Convert $2\frac{5}{8}$ to an improper fraction

$$2 \times 8 + 5 = 16 + 5 = 21$$

The denominator is 8. Therefore, $2\frac{5}{8} = \frac{21}{8}$

Example 9. Reduce $\frac{222}{37}$ to its lowest terms.

$$\frac{222}{37} = \frac{6 \times 37}{1 \times 37} = \frac{6}{1} \times \frac{37}{37} = 6 \times 1 = 6$$

EXERCISE 2.1

Reduce the following fractions to the lowest terms if possible.

1. $\dfrac{25}{50}$ = $\dfrac{1}{2}$

2. $\dfrac{10}{12}$ = $\dfrac{5}{6}$

3. $\dfrac{46}{16}$ = $\dfrac{23}{8}$ = $2\,^{7}/_{8}$ MIXED NO

4. $\dfrac{21}{12}$ = $\dfrac{7}{4}$

5. $\dfrac{8}{24}$ = $\dfrac{1}{3}$

6. $\dfrac{15}{26}$ = $\dfrac{15}{26}$

7. $\dfrac{6}{8}$ = $\dfrac{3}{4}$

8. $\dfrac{33}{121}$ = $\dfrac{3}{11}$

9. $\dfrac{200}{500}$ = $\dfrac{2}{5}$

10. $\dfrac{308}{187}$ = $\dfrac{28}{17}$ $\dfrac{28}{17}$

11. $\dfrac{92}{56}$ = $\dfrac{23}{14}$

12. $\dfrac{3150}{4158}$ = $\dfrac{150}{198}$ $\dfrac{126}{}$ $\dfrac{25}{33}$ ✓ ✓

   $25\overline{\smash{)}1575}$ 175
   $33\overline{\smash{)}2079}$ $231 : 7$

13. $\dfrac{102}{210}$ = $\dfrac{51}{105}$ $\dfrac{17}{35}$

14. $\dfrac{286}{858}$ = $\dfrac{1}{3}$

15. $\dfrac{48}{72}$ = $\dfrac{24}{36}$ $\dfrac{8}{12}$ $\dfrac{2}{3}$

16. $\dfrac{25}{80}$ = $\dfrac{5}{16}$

Convert the following mixed numbers to improper fractions.

17. $2\dfrac{1}{3}$ = $\dfrac{7}{3}$

18. $7\dfrac{1}{4}$ = $\dfrac{29}{4}$

19. $13\dfrac{2}{5}$ = $\dfrac{67}{5}$

20. $6\dfrac{1}{7}$ = $\dfrac{43}{7}$

21. $9\dfrac{11}{13}$ = $\dfrac{128}{13}$

22. $4\dfrac{8}{9}$ = $\dfrac{44}{9}$

Convert the following mixed numbers to improper fractions (continued).

23. $8\frac{1}{9}$ = $\frac{73}{9}$

24. $4\frac{3}{11}$ = $\frac{47}{11}$

25. $6\frac{2}{3}$ = $\frac{20}{3}$

26. $7\frac{1}{8}$ = $\frac{57}{8}$

27. $4\frac{3}{4}$ = $\frac{19}{4}$

28. $9\frac{2}{7}$ = $\frac{65}{7}$

29. $3\frac{1}{6}$ = $\frac{19}{6}$

30. $2\frac{7}{8}$ = $\frac{23}{8}$

31. $40\frac{5}{7}$ = $\frac{285}{7}$

32. $5\frac{1}{13}$ = $\frac{66}{13}$

Convert the following improper fractions to mixed numbers.

33. $\frac{11}{3}$ = $3\frac{2}{3}$

34. $\frac{49}{5}$ = $9\frac{4}{5}$

35. $\frac{9}{8}$ = $1\frac{1}{4}$

36. $\frac{100}{3}$ = $33\frac{1}{3}$

37. $\frac{68}{9}$ = $7\frac{5}{9}$

38. $\frac{31}{4}$ = $7\frac{3}{4}$

39. $\frac{31}{10}$ = $3\frac{1}{10}$

40. $\frac{8}{3}$ = $2\frac{2}{3}$

41. $\frac{87}{5}$ = $17\frac{2}{5}$

42. $\frac{53}{7}$ = $7\frac{4}{7}$

43. $\frac{111}{8}$ = $13\frac{7}{8}$

44. $\frac{55}{6}$ = $9\frac{1}{6}$

45. $\frac{143}{15}$ = $9\frac{8}{15}$

46. $\frac{267}{11}$ = $24\frac{3}{11}$

47. $\frac{93}{7}$ = $13\frac{2}{7}$

48. $\frac{436}{11}$ = $39\frac{7}{11}$

Answers to Exercise 2.1

1. $\frac{1}{2}$

2. $\frac{5}{6}$

3. $\frac{23}{8}$

4. $\frac{7}{4}$

5. $\frac{1}{3}$

6. $\frac{15}{26}$

7. $\frac{3}{4}$

8. $\frac{3}{11}$

9. $\frac{2}{5}$

10. $\frac{28}{17}$

11. $\frac{23}{14}$

12. $\frac{25}{33}$

13. $\frac{17}{35}$

14. $\frac{1}{3}$

15. $\frac{2}{3}$

16. $\frac{5}{16}$

17. $\frac{7}{3}$

18. $\frac{29}{4}$

19. $\frac{67}{5}$

20. $\frac{43}{7}$

21. $\frac{128}{13}$

22. $\frac{44}{9}$

23. $\frac{73}{9}$

24. $\frac{47}{11}$

25. $\frac{20}{3}$

26. $\frac{57}{8}$

27. $\frac{19}{4}$

28. $\frac{65}{7}$

29. $\frac{19}{6}$

30. $\frac{23}{8}$

31. $\frac{285}{7}$

32. $\frac{66}{13}$

33. $3\frac{2}{3}$

34. $9\frac{4}{5}$

35. $1\frac{1}{8}$

36. $33\frac{1}{3}$

37. $7\frac{5}{9}$

38. $7\frac{3}{4}$

39. $3\frac{1}{10}$

40. $2\frac{2}{3}$

41. $17\frac{2}{5}$

42. $7\frac{4}{7}$

43. $13\frac{7}{8}$

44. $9\frac{1}{6}$

45. $9\frac{8}{15}$

46. $24\frac{3}{11}$

47. $13\frac{2}{7}$

48. $39\frac{7}{11}$

2.2 Addition of Like Fractions

When adding two or more like fractions, we simply add their numerators and write the sum over the common denominator.

Example 1.

Add $\frac{2}{11} + \frac{5}{11}$. $\frac{2}{11} + \frac{5}{11} = \frac{7}{11}$

EXERCISE 2.2

Add each set of like fractions below and simplify your sum if possible. Express any improper fractions as a mixed number.

1. $\frac{1}{5} + \frac{2}{5} = ?$ $\frac{3}{5}$

4. $\frac{10}{19} + \frac{2}{19} + \frac{15}{19} = ?$ $1\frac{8}{19}$ 7. $\frac{2}{5} + 1\frac{3}{5}$ 2

2. $\frac{3}{22} + \frac{5}{22} = ?$ $\frac{8}{22}$

5. $\frac{7}{8} + \frac{2}{8} + \frac{5}{8} = ?$ $1\frac{6}{8}\frac{3}{4}$ HINT. First change the mixed mumber to an improper fraction.

3. $\frac{3}{17} + \frac{4}{17} + \frac{5}{17} = ?$ $\frac{13}{17}$

6. $\frac{1}{7} + \frac{3}{7} + \frac{5}{7} + \frac{6}{7} = ?$ $2\frac{1}{7}$ $1\frac{3}{5} = \frac{8}{5}$

Answers to Exercise 2.2
1. $\frac{3}{5}$ 2. $\frac{4}{11}$ 3. $\frac{12}{17}$ 4. $1\frac{8}{19}$ 5. $1\frac{3}{4}$ 6. $2\frac{1}{7}$ 7. $\frac{10}{5}$ or 2

2.3 Lowest Common Denominator

When adding two or more unlike fractions, we must first find a *lowest common denominator (LCD)*. The LCD is the smallest whole number that is exactly divisible by all of the denominators.

Example 1.   Find the LCD of the fractions $\frac{1}{15}, \frac{1}{5}, \frac{1}{8}$.

The LCD is 120, because 120 is the smallest whole number divisible by 5, 8, and 15.

We cannot always determine the LCD by inspection. Before we look at the procedure it is important to understand what is meant by a *prime number* A prime number is a whole number whose only factors are 1 and itself. For example, 2, 3, 5, 7, and 11 are prime numbers. Two or more numbers being multiplied are called *factors*. Note that 6 is not a prime number because it has factors other than 1 and 6, namely 2 and 3. Whole numbers which are not prime are called *composite*.

The procedure for finding an LCD is as follows.
1. Factor each denominator into its prime factors; that is, factor each number completely.
2. For each prime factor, look for the denominator in which it appears the most times. Write each factor the number of times it appears most in any one denominator in Step 1.
3. Multiply together the prime factors listed in Step 2. The product is the LCD.

Example 2.

Find the LCD of $\dfrac{4}{27}$ and $\dfrac{5}{18}$.

Step 1: $\quad 27 = 3 \times 9$
$\qquad\qquad = 3 \times 3 \times 3$
$\qquad\quad 18 = 2 \times 9$
$\qquad\qquad = 2 \times 3 \times 3$

Step 2: $\quad (3 \times 3 \times 3) \times (2)$

Step 3: $\quad 3 \times 3 \times 3 \times 2 = 54$

The LCD is 54.

Exercise 2.3

Find the LCD for each of the sets of fractions.

1. $\dfrac{3}{8}, \dfrac{2}{5}$

2. $\dfrac{4}{7}, \dfrac{1}{3}, \dfrac{17}{49}$

3. $\dfrac{5}{27}, \dfrac{2}{3}, \dfrac{11}{12}$

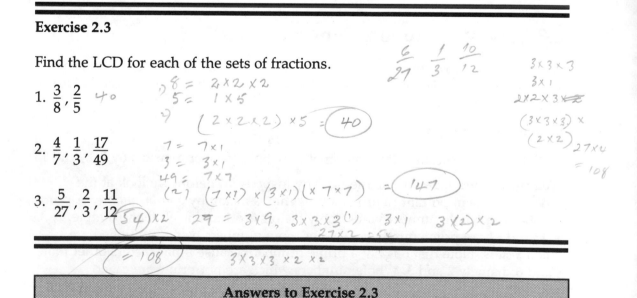

Answers to Exercise 2.3		
1. 40	2. 147	3. 108

2.4 Addition of Unlike Fractions

Suppose we want to add $\frac{4}{5}$ and $\frac{2}{3}$. Since these fractions are unlike, we must first change them to equivalent fractions that have a common denominator. This means that we need to find the LCD of 5 and 3. The LCD is 15. We then convert $\frac{4}{5}$ into an equivalent fraction having a denominator of 15. We do the same with $\frac{2}{3}$.

$$\frac{4}{5} = \frac{12}{15} \text{ and } \frac{2}{3} = \frac{10}{15}$$

We then add the equivalent fractions.

$$\frac{4}{5} + \frac{2}{3} = \frac{12}{15} + \frac{10}{15}$$
$$= \frac{12 + 10}{15}$$
$$= \frac{22}{15} \text{ or } 1\frac{7}{15}$$

Note that when we convert $\frac{4}{5}$ to $\frac{12}{15}$ we are simply multiplying $\frac{4}{5}$ by 1, but 1 is written as $\frac{3}{3}$. Multiplying any number by 1 doesn't change its value, but it may change its appearance.

$$\frac{4}{5} = \frac{4 \times 1}{5}$$
$$= \frac{4}{5} \times \frac{3}{3}$$
$$= \frac{4 \times 3}{5 \times 3}$$
$$= \frac{12}{15}$$

Example 1. Add $\frac{1}{8} + \frac{5}{32}$.

Find the LCD: 32

$$\frac{1}{8} + \frac{5}{32} = \frac{4}{32} + \frac{5}{32}$$
$$= \frac{9}{32}$$

Example 2. Add $\frac{5}{18} + \frac{11}{12}$.

Find the LCD. $18 = 2 \times 3 \times 3$
$12 = 2 \times 2 \times 3$

$$LCD = 2 \times 2 \times 3 \times 3$$
$$= 36$$
$$\frac{5}{18} + \frac{11}{12} = \frac{10}{36} + \frac{33}{36}$$
$$= \frac{43}{36} \text{ or } 1\frac{7}{36}$$

$3 \times 5 \times 7 \times 3 = 315$

$\begin{array}{l} 210 \\ 189 \\ 225 \\ 245 \end{array}$ $\dfrac{869}{315}$

Exercise 2.4

Add the following unlike fractions and express your answer in simplest form.

1. $\dfrac{2}{9} + \dfrac{5}{18}$ $9 = 3 \times 3$ $LCD = 2 \times 3 \times 3 = 18$

$18 = 2 \times 3 \times 3$ $\dfrac{4 + 5}{18} = 9/18 = 1/2$

2. $\dfrac{2}{5} + \dfrac{5}{6} + \dfrac{1}{2}$ $5 = 1 \times 5$
$6 = 2 \times 2 \times 2$ or 2×3 $5 \times 2 \times 3 = LCD \ 30$ $\dfrac{12 + 25 + 15}{30}$ $\dfrac{52}{30}$ or $1\dfrac{22}{30}$

3. $\dfrac{2}{15} + \dfrac{3}{4} + \dfrac{1}{16}$ $5 \times 3 = LCD$ $\dfrac{6+}{15}$ $= \dfrac{26}{15}$ or $1\dfrac{11}{15}$

$5 \times 3 \times 2 \times 2 \times 2 \quad \dfrac{32+180+15}{125} \dfrac{228}{240} \quad \dfrac{114}{120} \dfrac{57}{60} \quad \dfrac{227}{240}$

4. $\dfrac{2}{3} + \dfrac{3}{5} + \dfrac{5}{7} + \dfrac{7}{9}$ $3 \times 5 \times 7 \times 3$ $\dfrac{210 + 189 + 225 + 245}{315}$ $\dfrac{869}{315} = 2\dfrac{239}{315}$

5. If a share of stock gained $\dfrac{5}{8}$ of a point during one day of trading and $\dfrac{3}{7}$ of a point of the next day of trading, how many points did the stock gain during those two days? $\dfrac{5}{8} + \dfrac{3}{7}$ $2 \times 2 \times 2 \times 7$ $\dfrac{35 + 24}{56}$

6. $\dfrac{2}{7} + \dfrac{3}{7} = ?$ $\dfrac{5}{7}$

13. $3\dfrac{1}{2} + 2\dfrac{1}{3} = ?$ $\dfrac{21 + 14}{6} = 3\dfrac{5}{6}$ $5\dfrac{5}{6}$ ✓

7. $\dfrac{15}{17} + \dfrac{3}{17} = ?$ $1\dfrac{1}{17}$

14. $6\dfrac{2}{3} + 8\dfrac{2}{3} = ?$ $\dfrac{20 + 26}{3} \dfrac{46}{3}$ $15\dfrac{1}{3}$

8. $\dfrac{2}{3} + \dfrac{1}{2} + \dfrac{5}{6} = ?$

15. $11\dfrac{1}{9} + 3 = ?$ $\dfrac{100}{9} + 3 = 14\dfrac{1}{9}$

9. $\dfrac{5}{18} + \dfrac{11}{12} = ?$ $\dfrac{43}{36}$ $1\dfrac{7}{36}$

16. $4\dfrac{3}{5} + \dfrac{1}{2} = ?$ $\dfrac{46 + 5}{10}$ $\dfrac{51}{10}$ $5\dfrac{1}{10}$

10. $\dfrac{4}{11} + \dfrac{5}{9} + \dfrac{6}{7} = ?$

17. $2\dfrac{1}{2} + 3\dfrac{1}{3} + 4\dfrac{1}{4} = ?$ $\dfrac{60 + 80 + 102}{24} \dfrac{242}{24}$

11. $\dfrac{3}{7} + \dfrac{5}{7} + \dfrac{7}{9} + \dfrac{2}{3} = ?$

18. $9\dfrac{2}{7} + 4\dfrac{3}{4} = ?$ $\dfrac{336}{28}$

12. $\dfrac{13}{15} + \dfrac{5}{36} = ?$

19. $3\dfrac{1}{4} + 2\dfrac{1}{3} + 4\dfrac{3}{5} = ?$ $\dfrac{195 + 140 + 276}{60}$ $\dfrac{611}{60}$

$10\dfrac{11}{60}$ ✓

$\dfrac{65}{7} + \dfrac{19}{4} \quad \dfrac{260 + 133}{28} = \dfrac{393}{28} \quad 14\dfrac{1}{28}$

Answers to Exercise 2.4

1. $\dfrac{1}{2}$

2. $\dfrac{26}{15}$ or $1\dfrac{11}{15}$

3. $\dfrac{227}{240}$

4. $2\dfrac{239}{315}$

5. $1\dfrac{3}{56}$

6. $\dfrac{5}{7}$

7. $\dfrac{18}{17}$ or $1\dfrac{1}{17}$

8. 2

9. $\dfrac{43}{36}$ or $1\dfrac{7}{36}$

10. $\dfrac{1231}{693}$ or $1\dfrac{538}{693}$

11. $\dfrac{869}{315}$ or $2\dfrac{239}{315}$

12. $\dfrac{181}{180}$ or $1\dfrac{1}{180}$

13. $5\dfrac{5}{6}$

14. $15\dfrac{1}{3}$

15. $14\dfrac{1}{9}$

16. $5\dfrac{1}{10}$

17. $10\dfrac{1}{12}$

18. $14\dfrac{1}{28}$

19. $10\dfrac{11}{60}$

2.5 Subtraction of Fractions

The process of subtracting fractions is similar to the addition of fractions. To subtract like fractions, simply subtract the smaller numerator from the larger numerator, place the difference over the common denominator and simplify if possible.

Example 1. Subtract $\dfrac{17}{32} - \dfrac{5}{32}$.

$$\dfrac{17}{32} - \dfrac{5}{32} = \dfrac{17-5}{32}$$
$$= \dfrac{12}{32} \text{ or } \dfrac{3}{8}$$

Example 2. Subtract $\dfrac{7}{13}$ from $\dfrac{12}{13}$.

$$\dfrac{12}{13} - \dfrac{7}{13} = \dfrac{12-7}{13}$$
$$= \dfrac{5}{13}$$

If we are subtracting unlike fractions, we must first find the LCD, just as we did when adding unlike fractions.

Example 3. Subtract $\dfrac{4}{11} - \dfrac{3}{9}$.

The LCD is 99.

$$\dfrac{4}{11} - \dfrac{3}{9} = \dfrac{36}{99} - \dfrac{33}{99}$$
$$= \dfrac{36-33}{99}$$
$$= \dfrac{3}{99}$$
$$= \dfrac{1}{33}$$

Example 4. Subtract $\dfrac{7}{5}$ from $\dfrac{21}{13}$.

The LCD is 65.

$$\dfrac{21}{13} - \dfrac{7}{5} = \dfrac{105}{65} - \dfrac{91}{65}$$
$$= \dfrac{105-91}{65}$$
$$= \dfrac{14}{65}$$

38

EXERCISE 2.5

Subtract the following fractions.

1. $\dfrac{11}{17} - \dfrac{5}{17}$ $\dfrac{6}{17}$

2. $\dfrac{21}{13} - \dfrac{7}{5}$ $\dfrac{14}{65}$

3. $\dfrac{4}{5} - \dfrac{2}{3}$ $\dfrac{12-10}{15} = \dfrac{2}{15}$

4. $\dfrac{10}{17} - \dfrac{5}{11}$ $\dfrac{17}{170}{187}$ $\dfrac{110-85}{187}$ $\dfrac{25}{187}$

5. In a new business condominium, $\frac{2}{3}$ of the building is occupied by the Ajax Hardware Co., and $\frac{1}{5}$ of the building is occupied by Belair Realty. How much of the building is *not* occupied? $\dfrac{10+3=13}{15}$ $\dfrac{2}{3} - \dfrac{1}{5}$ $\dfrac{10+3}{15} = \dfrac{3}{13}$ ✓

6. $\dfrac{9}{16} - \dfrac{4}{16} = ?$ $\dfrac{5}{16}$

7. $\dfrac{5}{12} - \dfrac{1}{3} = ?$ $\dfrac{5-4}{12} = \dfrac{1}{12} = \dfrac{3}{8}$

8. $\dfrac{1}{2} - \dfrac{3}{6} = ?$ $\dfrac{3-3}{6} = 0$

9. $\dfrac{3}{4} - \dfrac{1}{6} = ?$ $\dfrac{18-4}{24} = \dfrac{14}{24}\dfrac{7}{12}$

10. $5\dfrac{1}{3} - 2\dfrac{7}{8} = ?$ $\dfrac{16/3 - 3\frac{5}{8}}{24}$

11. $10\dfrac{5}{6} - 3\dfrac{3}{6} = ?$ $\dfrac{65/6 \div 21/6}{6} = \dfrac{65-21}{6}$ $\dfrac{44}{6} = \dfrac{22}{3} 7\frac{1}{3}$

12. $39\dfrac{1}{6} - \dfrac{5}{7} = ?$ $\dfrac{235}{6}$ $\dfrac{160/5}{42} - 30 = \dfrac{160/5}{42}$ $38\dfrac{19}{42}$

13. $17\dfrac{11}{13} - 9 = ?$ $8\dfrac{11}{13}$

14. $(5\dfrac{1}{3} - 3\dfrac{1}{4}) + 4\dfrac{1}{5} = ?$ $\dfrac{(\frac{16}{3} - \frac{13}{4} 64-39)}{12}$ $29\frac{1}{5}$ $\dfrac{25}{12} = 2\frac{1}{12}$

15. $7\dfrac{2}{9} - (1\dfrac{7}{8} + 3\dfrac{1}{4}) = ?$

(*HINT*: Perform operations within parenthesis first)

$\dfrac{604}{288}$ $\dfrac{302}{144}$ $\dfrac{151}{72}$

$2\dfrac{7}{72}$ ✓

$\dfrac{256-75}{128-15} = \dfrac{181}{24}$ $7\dfrac{7}{24}$

$5\frac{1}{3} - 3\frac{1}{4} = \dfrac{16/3 - 13/4}{12}$

$= \dfrac{64-39}{12}$

$7\dfrac{2}{9} - \left(1\dfrac{7}{8} + 3\dfrac{1}{4}\right)$ $\dfrac{\frac{15}{8} + \frac{13}{4}}{32}$ $\dfrac{253}{24}$ $2\dfrac{5}{24}$

$\dfrac{65}{9} - \dfrac{164}{32} \dfrac{2080-1476}{288} = \dfrac{60+104}{32}$ $\dfrac{164}{32}$ $= 2\dfrac{11}{24}$ ✓

$= \dfrac{25}{12} + \dfrac{21}{5} = \dfrac{125+252}{60} \dfrac{377}{60}$

$= 6\dfrac{17}{60}$

Answers to Exercise 2.5

1. $\frac{6}{17}$

2. $\frac{14}{65}$

3. $\frac{2}{15}$

4. $\frac{25}{187}$

5. $\frac{2}{15}$

6. $\frac{5}{16}$

7. $\frac{1}{12}$

8. 0

9. $\frac{7}{12}$

10. $2\frac{11}{24}$

11. $7\frac{1}{3}$

12. $38\frac{19}{42}$

13. $8\frac{11}{13}$

14. $6\frac{17}{60}$

15. $2\frac{7}{72}$

2.6 Multiplication of Fractions

There is no need to find an LCD when we multiply fractions. To find the product of two fractions, first multiply their numerators. This product will be the numerator of the new fraction. Then multiply their denominators. This product will be the denominator of the new fraction. If it is possible to reduce your answer to lower terms, do so.

In general:

$$\frac{a}{b} \times \frac{c}{d} = \frac{a \times c}{b \times d}$$

where b and d do not equal zero.

Example 1. Multiply $\frac{3}{5} \times \frac{4}{7}$.

$$\frac{3}{5} \times \frac{4}{7} = \frac{3 \times 4}{5 \times 7}$$
$$= \frac{12}{35}$$

Example 2. Multiply $\frac{2}{9} \times \frac{5}{14}$.

$$\frac{2}{9} \times \frac{5}{14} = \frac{2 \times 5}{9 \times 14}$$
$$= \frac{10}{126}$$
$$= \frac{5}{63} \quad \text{reduced to lowest terms}$$

Example 3. $\frac{4}{5} \times 3\frac{3}{8}$

HINT: First convert the mixed number to an improper fraction. $3\frac{3}{8} = \frac{27}{8}$

$$\frac{4}{5} \times \frac{27}{8} = \frac{4 \times 27}{5 \times 8}$$
$$= \frac{27}{10}$$

EXERCISE 2.6

Multiply the following fractions and express your answer in simplest form.

1. $\frac{1}{5} \times \frac{2}{7}$ $\frac{1 \times 2}{5 \times 7} = \frac{2}{35}$

2. $\frac{5}{13} \times \frac{4}{9}$ $\frac{20}{117}$

3. $\frac{1}{7} \times \frac{2}{3} \times \frac{6}{5}$ $\frac{12}{105}$ $\frac{4}{35}$

4. $\frac{6}{7} \times (\frac{2}{9} + \frac{3}{4})$ $\frac{2/9 + 3/4}{36}$ $\frac{8+27}{36}$ $\frac{35}{36}$
   $\frac{6}{7} \times \frac{35}{36}$ $\frac{210}{252}$ $\frac{30}{36}$ $\frac{10}{12}$ $\frac{5}{6}$

5. $\frac{3}{8} \times \frac{2}{5}$ $\frac{6}{40}$ $\frac{3}{20}$

6. $\frac{1}{2} \times \frac{5}{6}$ $\frac{5}{12}$

7. $\frac{1}{10} \times \frac{3}{8}$ $\frac{3}{80}$

8. $\frac{5}{6} \times \frac{2}{15}$ $\frac{10}{90} = \frac{1}{9}$

9. $\frac{5}{12} \times \frac{42}{65}$ $\frac{210}{780}$ $\frac{21}{78}$ $\frac{7}{26}$

10. $\frac{8}{3} \times \frac{21}{32}$ $\frac{168}{96} = \frac{56}{32}$ $\frac{28}{16}$ $\frac{14}{8}$ $\frac{7}{4}$ $1\frac{3}{4}$

11. $\frac{5}{6} \times 40$ $\frac{200}{6} = \frac{100}{3} = 33\frac{1}{3}$

12. $9 \times 3\frac{1}{3}$ $\frac{9 \times 10}{1 \times 3}$ $\frac{90}{3} = 30$

13. $5\frac{2}{3} \times 12$ $\frac{17}{3} \times 12$ $\frac{204}{3}$ $\frac{68}{1}$

14. $3\frac{1}{3} \times 6\frac{3}{5}$ $\frac{10}{3} \times \frac{33}{5} = \frac{330}{15}$ $= 22$

15. $2\frac{1}{5} \times \frac{5}{22}$ $\frac{11}{5} \times \frac{5}{22}$ $\frac{55}{110}$ $\frac{11}{25}$ $\frac{1}{2}$

16. $3\frac{1}{7} \times 2\frac{1}{8}$ $\frac{22}{7} \times \frac{17}{8}$ $\frac{374}{56}$ $\frac{187}{28}$ $6\frac{19}{28}$

17. $4\frac{7}{8} \times 0 = 0$

18. $11\frac{1}{3} \times 7\frac{3}{34}$ $\frac{34}{3} \times \frac{241}{34}$ $\frac{8194}{102}$ $80\frac{34}{102}$ $80\frac{1}{3}$

19. $5\frac{3}{8} \times 6\frac{2}{5}$ $\frac{43}{8} \times \frac{32}{5}$ $\frac{1376}{40}$ $\frac{344}{10}$ $\frac{172}{5}$ $34\frac{2}{5}$

20. $\frac{16}{85} \times \frac{125}{84}$ $\frac{2000}{7140}$ $\frac{100}{357}$ ✓

21. $\frac{3}{7} \times (\frac{4}{5} + \frac{3}{4})$ $\frac{3}{7} \times (\frac{4/5 + 3/4}{20})$ $\frac{16+15}{20} = \frac{31}{20} \times \frac{7}{7}$
    $= \frac{93}{140}$ ✓

22. $(\frac{2}{9} - \frac{1}{7}) \times (\frac{1}{3} + \frac{2}{5})$ $\frac{14-9}{63}$ $\frac{5}{63} \times \frac{2}{15}$ $\frac{10}{945}$ $\frac{2}{189}$

23. $\frac{5}{7} \times \frac{14}{25} \times \frac{21}{28}$ $\frac{1470}{4900}$ $\frac{21}{70}$ $\frac{3}{10}$

$\frac{2/9 - 1/7}{63}$ $\frac{14-9}{63}$ $(\frac{5}{63}) \times \frac{11}{15}$ $\frac{1/3 + 2/5}{15}$ $\frac{5+6}{15}$ $(\frac{11}{15})$ $\frac{55}{945}$ $\frac{11}{189}$

$$\frac{3}{7} \times \left(\frac{4}{5} + \frac{3}{4}\right) \qquad \frac{16+15}{20} \qquad \frac{31}{20} \times \frac{3}{7} \qquad \frac{93}{140}$$

$$\left(\frac{2}{9} - \frac{1}{7}\right) \times \left(\frac{1}{3} + \frac{2}{5}\right) \qquad \frac{14-9}{63} \qquad \frac{5}{63} \times \left(\frac{5+6}{15}\right) = \frac{11}{15} \qquad \frac{55}{945} \quad \frac{11}{189} \quad \checkmark$$

Answers to Exercise 2.6

1. $\frac{2}{35}$ ✓

2. $\frac{20}{117}$ ✓

3. $\frac{4}{35}$ ✓

4. $\frac{5}{6}$ ✓

5. $\frac{3}{20}$ ✓

6. $\frac{5}{12}$ ✓

7. $\frac{3}{80}$ ✓

8. $\frac{1}{9}$ ✓

9. $\frac{7}{26}$ ✓

10. $\frac{7}{4}$ ✓

11. $\frac{100}{3}$ or $33\frac{1}{3}$ ✓

12. 30 ✓

13. 68 ✓

14. 22 ✓

15. $\frac{1}{2}$ ✓

16. $6\frac{19}{28}$ ✓

17. 0 ✓

18. $80\frac{1}{3}$ ✓

19. $34\frac{2}{5}$ ✓

20. $\frac{100}{357}$ ✓

21. $\frac{93}{140}$ ✓

22. $\frac{11}{189}$ ✓

23. $\frac{3}{10}$ ✓

2.7 Division of Fractions

When we divide by a fraction, we first invert the fraction. We then multiply by the inverted fraction. In general,

$$\frac{a}{b} \div \frac{c}{d} = \frac{a}{b} \times \frac{d}{c}$$

if b, c, and d are not equal to zero.

Example 1. Divide $\frac{2}{3} \div \frac{3}{5}$.

$$\frac{2}{3} \div \frac{3}{5} = \frac{2}{3} \times \frac{5}{3}$$

$$= \frac{10}{9} \text{ or } 1\frac{1}{9}$$

Let's consider the above example in more detail. We can write $\frac{2}{3} \div \frac{3}{5}$ as $\left(\frac{2}{3} \div \frac{3}{5}\right) \times 1$

Remember that 1 multiplied times any number is that number. And since 1 is any nonzero number divided by itself, we can replace the 1 with $(\frac{5}{3} \div \frac{5}{3})$

Therefore: $\frac{2}{3} \div \frac{3}{5} = (\frac{2}{3} \div \frac{3}{5}) \times (\frac{5}{3} \div \frac{5}{3})$

or
$= \frac{2}{3} \div \frac{3}{5} \times \frac{10}{6} \div \frac{10}{6}$

$$= \frac{\frac{2}{3}}{\frac{3}{5}} \times \frac{\frac{5}{3}}{\frac{5}{3}}$$

$= \dfrac{\frac{2}{3} \cdot \frac{5}{3}}{\frac{10}{6} \quad \frac{10}{6}}$

But $\frac{3}{5} \times \frac{5}{3} = \frac{15}{15} = 1$. Therefore

But $\frac{10}{6} \times \frac{10}{6} = \frac{100}{36}$ ∴ *why did they choose 5/3?*

$$\frac{2}{3} \div \frac{3}{5} = \frac{\frac{2}{3} \times \frac{3}{5}}{1} = \frac{2}{3} \times \frac{3}{5}$$

Example 2. Divide $\frac{4}{7}$ by $\frac{2}{5}$.

$$\frac{4}{7} \div \frac{2}{5} = \frac{4}{7} \times \frac{5}{2}$$
$$= \frac{20}{14}$$
$$= \frac{10}{7} \text{ or } 1\frac{3}{7}$$

Example 3. Divide $\frac{3}{7} \div \frac{1}{4}$.

$$\frac{3}{7} \div \frac{1}{4} = \frac{3}{7} \times \frac{4}{1}$$
$$= \frac{12}{7} \text{ or } 1\frac{5}{7}$$

Example 4. Divide $\frac{21}{25}$ by $\frac{3}{5}$.

$$\frac{21}{25} \div \frac{3}{5} = \frac{21}{25} \times \frac{5}{3}$$
$$= \frac{105}{75}$$
$$= \frac{7}{5} \text{ or } 1\frac{2}{5}$$

Example 5. Divide $\frac{7}{3}$ by $3\frac{1}{3}$.

$$\frac{7}{3} \div 3\frac{1}{3} = \frac{5}{3} \div \frac{10}{3}$$
$$= \frac{7}{3} \times \frac{3}{10}$$
$$= \frac{21}{30}$$
$$= \frac{7}{10}$$

It would be useful to simplify our numbers before we multiplied:

$$\frac{21}{25} \div \frac{3}{5} = \frac{21}{25} \times \frac{5}{3} = \frac{7}{5} \times \frac{1}{1} = \frac{7}{5}$$

$\frac{105}{75}$

EXERCISE 2.7

Divide the following fractions and express your answer in simplest form.

1. $\dfrac{2}{3} \div \dfrac{1}{2}$ $\frac{2}{3} \times \frac{2}{1} = \frac{4}{3} = 1\frac{1}{3}$

9. $8 \div \dfrac{3}{4}$ $\frac{8}{1} \div \frac{3}{4} = \frac{8}{1} \times \frac{4}{3}$ $\frac{32}{3}$ $10\frac{2}{3}$

2. $\dfrac{23}{3} \div \dfrac{11}{2}$ $\frac{23}{3} \times \frac{2}{11} = \frac{46}{33}$

10. $\dfrac{3}{4} \div 8$ $\frac{3}{4} \div \frac{8}{1}$ $\frac{3}{4} \times \frac{1}{8}$ $\frac{3}{32}$

3. $\dfrac{18}{25} \div 4$ (recall that $4 = \dfrac{4}{1}$) $\frac{18}{25} \times \frac{1}{4}$ $\frac{18}{100}$ $\frac{9}{50}$ ✓

11. $\dfrac{1}{3} \div \dfrac{1}{9}$ $\frac{1}{3} \times \frac{9}{1}$ $\frac{9}{3}$ 3

4. $\dfrac{0}{7} \div \dfrac{5}{17}$ $\frac{0}{7} \times \frac{17}{5} = \frac{17}{35}$ $8^2/5$ 0

12. $16 \div \dfrac{24}{31}$ $\frac{16}{1} \times \frac{31}{24}$ $\frac{496}{24}$ $\frac{62}{3}$ $\frac{62}{3}$ ✓

5. $\dfrac{4}{7} \div \dfrac{5}{6}$ $\frac{4}{7} \times \frac{6}{5}$ $\frac{24}{35}$ ·

13. $\dfrac{3}{8} \div 2\dfrac{3}{4}$ $\frac{3}{8} \div \frac{11}{4}$ $\frac{3}{8} \times \frac{4}{11}$ $\frac{12}{88}$ $\frac{3}{22}$ $\frac{6}{44}$ $\boxed{\frac{3}{22}}$

6. $\dfrac{3}{4} \div \dfrac{0}{2}$ $\frac{3}{4} \times \frac{2}{0} = \emptyset$

14. $6\dfrac{9}{16} \div 1\dfrac{3}{32}$ ✓ $\frac{105}{16} \div \frac{35}{32}$ $\frac{105}{16} \times \frac{32}{35}$ $\frac{3360}{560} = 6$ ✓

7. $\dfrac{3}{7} \div \dfrac{2}{3}$ $\frac{3}{7} \times \frac{3}{2}$ $\frac{9}{14}$

15. $\left(3\dfrac{2}{7} \div 4\dfrac{1}{9} \right) \div 2\dfrac{5}{7}$ $\frac{23}{7} \div \frac{37}{9} = \frac{23}{7} \times \frac{9}{37} = \frac{207}{259}$ ✓ $\div \frac{19}{7}$ $\frac{207}{259} \times \frac{7}{19}$ $\frac{1449}{4921}$ ✓ $\frac{207}{703}$

8. $\dfrac{3}{5} \div \dfrac{12}{25}$ $\frac{3}{5} \times \frac{25}{12}$ $\frac{75}{60}$ $\frac{15}{12}$ $1\frac{3}{12}$

$= 1\frac{1}{4}$

16. $7\dfrac{1}{9} \div \left(\dfrac{6}{7} \div 7\dfrac{1}{6} \right)$

$\frac{64}{9} \div$ $\frac{6}{7} \div \frac{43}{6}$ $\left(\frac{6}{7} \times \frac{6}{43} \right)$ $\frac{36}{301}$

$\frac{3}{8} \times \frac{100}{300}$ $\frac{300}{8}$ ×

$\frac{3}{8} \div 2\frac{3}{4}$

1.7

$= \frac{3}{8} \div \frac{11}{4}$

$\frac{4.6875}{2.75}$

$= \frac{3}{8} \times \frac{4}{11}$ $\frac{12}{88}$ $\frac{6}{44}$ $\boxed{\frac{3}{22}}$

$\frac{64}{9} \times \frac{301}{36}$ $\frac{19264}{324}$

$\frac{9632}{162}$ $\frac{4816}{81}$

$59\frac{37}{81}$ ✓

44

Answers to Exercise 2.7

1. $\frac{4}{3}$ or $1\frac{1}{3}$

2. $\frac{46}{33}$

3. $\frac{9}{50}$

4. 0

5. $\frac{24}{35}$

6. Impossible: can't divide by zero.

7. $\frac{9}{14}$

8. $\frac{5}{4}$ or $1\frac{1}{4}$

9. $\frac{32}{3}$ or $10\frac{2}{3}$

10. $\frac{3}{32}$

11. 3

12. $\frac{62}{3}$ or $20\frac{2}{3}$

13. $\frac{3}{11}$ 3/22 ?

14. 6

15. $\frac{207}{703}$ ✓

16. $59\frac{37}{81}$

3.0 DECIMALS

We encounter decimals each time we make a purchase or receive a paycheck. The operations of addition, subtraction, multiplication, and division are all applicable to decimal numbers.

If a decimal number is greater than one, say 23.45, we read the digits to the left of the decimal point as whole numbers. The decimal point is read as "and," and the digits to the right of the decimal point are read as a fraction using the place value of the extreme right digit as the denominator. Thus, 23.45 is read as "23 and 45 hundredths." Alternatively, we can read it as "twenty-three point four five."

Example 1. Write these decimals in words: (a) 12.3, (b) 1.23, and (c) 0.123.

(a) 12.3 is twelve and three tenths.

(b) 1.23 is one and twenty-three hundredths.

(c) 0.123 is one hundred twenty-three thousandths.

3.1 Converting Fractions to Decimals

Any fraction can be expressed as a decimal by simply dividing the denominator into the numerator.

Example 2. Use a calculator to convert these fractions to decimals: (a) $\frac{3}{5}$, (b) $\frac{11}{17}$, and (c) $\frac{1}{3}$.

(a) | 3 | ÷ | 5 | = | 0.6

(b) | 11 | ÷ | 17 | = | 0.6470588

(c) | 1 | ÷ | 3 | = | 0.3333333

This is called a repeating decimal.

=====

EXERCISE 3.1

Convert the following fractions to an equivalent decimal number. Express answer correct to the nearest hundredth.

1. $\dfrac{4}{5}$ .8

2. $8\dfrac{3}{4}$ 8.75

3. $\dfrac{7}{500}$ .014

4. $\dfrac{87}{100}$ .87

5. $72\dfrac{11}{25}$ 72.44

6. $\dfrac{6}{8}$ .75

7. $\dfrac{5}{9}$ .55 = .56

8. $\dfrac{1}{3}$ .3333

9. $\dfrac{7}{12}$ .58

10. $\dfrac{1}{4}$ .25

11. $\dfrac{9}{10}$ .90

12. $\dfrac{25}{32}$ .78.25 .78

13. $\dfrac{27}{135}$ .29409 .2

14. $\dfrac{5}{11}$ .4545

15. $\dfrac{7}{9}$ .7777 .78

=====

Answers to Exercise 3.1

1. 0.80	6. 0.75	11. 0.90
2. 8.75	7. 0.56	12. 0.78
3. 0.01	8. 0.33	13. 0.20
4. 0.87	9. 0.58	14. 0.45
5. 72.44	10. 0.25	15. 0.78

3.2 Converting Decimals to Fractions

If any common fraction can be changed to an equivalent decimal number, isn't it reasonable to assume that any decimal number could be changed to a common fraction? If $\frac{3}{5}$ = 0.6, then 0.6 = $\frac{3}{5}$. Since 0.6 is six-tenths,

$$0.6 = \frac{6}{10}$$
$$= \frac{3}{5}$$

We can change any decimal fraction to its equivalent common fraction by first determining the place value of the digit on the extreme right, and using that value as the denominator of our common fraction. For example:

0.24

4's place value is hundredths. Thus, the denominator of our fraction is 100. The digits in the decimal fraction, in this case 24, is the numerator of your fraction. Hence,

$0.24 = \frac{24}{100}$ which can be reduced to $\frac{6}{25}$

Similarly, $0.625 = \frac{625}{1000}$ or $\frac{5}{8}$

and $5.13 = \frac{513}{100}$

48

EXERCISE 3.2

Convert the following decimal fractions to an equivalent common fraction in simplest form:

1. 0.002 $\quad = \frac{2}{1000} = \frac{1}{500}$

2. 0.76 $\quad = \frac{76}{100} \quad \frac{38}{50} \quad \frac{19}{25}$ ✓

3. 1.65 (Hint: $1\frac{65}{100}$) $\quad \frac{165}{100} \quad \frac{13}{2} \quad 6\frac{1}{2} \quad 1.65 = 1\frac{65}{100} \quad \frac{165}{100} \quad \frac{33}{20}$

4. 0.09 $\quad \frac{9}{100}$

5. 0.085 $\quad .085 = \frac{85}{1000} \quad \frac{17}{200}$

6. 0.17 $\quad \frac{17}{100}$

7. 0.123 $\quad \frac{123}{1000}$

8. 2.3 $\quad 2.3 = 2\frac{3}{10} = \frac{23}{10}$

9. 17.06 $\quad 17.06 = 17 \times 100 + \frac{6}{100} \quad \frac{176}{100} \quad \frac{88}{50} \quad \frac{1706}{100} = \frac{853}{150}$

10. 2.576 $\quad 2.576 \quad \frac{576}{1000} \quad \frac{2576}{1000} \quad \frac{1288}{500} \quad \frac{604}{200} \quad \frac{322}{125}$

11. 0.0037 $\quad .0037$ $\quad \frac{}{10000}$

12. 260.26 $\quad 260.\frac{26000}{26} \quad 260.\frac{26}{100} \quad \frac{2606}{100} \quad \frac{1313}{50} \qquad \frac{10003}{5000}$

13. 0.871 $\quad .871$ $\quad \frac{}{1000}$ $\qquad \frac{20006}{10000}$

14. 3.75 $\quad 3.75 = 3\frac{75}{100} \quad 3\frac{75}{100} \quad \frac{75}{20} \quad \frac{15}{4} \qquad 2.\frac{006}{1000}$

15. 2.006 $\quad 2.\frac{006}{1000} \quad \frac{2006}{1000} \quad \frac{1003}{}$

Answers to Exercise 3.2

1. $\dfrac{1}{500}$ 9. $\dfrac{853}{50}$

2. $\dfrac{19}{25}$ 10. $\dfrac{322}{125}$

3. $\dfrac{33}{20}$ 11. $\dfrac{37}{10,000}$

4. $\dfrac{9}{100}$ 12. $\dfrac{13,013}{50}$

5. $\dfrac{17}{200}$ 13. $\dfrac{871}{1000}$

6. $\dfrac{17}{100}$ 14. $\dfrac{15}{4}$

7. $\dfrac{123}{1000}$ 15. $\dfrac{20006}{10000}$ $\dfrac{10003}{5000}$

8. $\dfrac{23}{10}$

3.3 Adding Decimal Numbers

Adding decimal numbers is not much different from adding whole numbers. We need to arrange the decimal numbers under each other, keeping the decimal points aligned in a vertical column. Once this is done, add as if they were whole numbers.

For example:

Add the following: 2.134 + 51.02 + 0.0394

```
  2.134
 51.02
  0.0394
 53.1934
```

50

EXERCISE 3.3

Add the following decimal numbers. Check your answers using your calculator.

1. 103 + 236.1 + 0.067

2. 0.5 + 51 + .51

3. 1.234 + 12.34 + 123.4 + 123

4. Tom needs to pay the following monthly bills: rent, $289; car payment, $137.49; groceries, $201.35; E-Z credit card payment, $72.12. What is Tom's total monthly payment?

5. The following deposits were made in a local environmental organization's bank account: $463.62, $74.89, $111.10, and $59.89. If the account had a previous balance of $1,593.43, what is the new balance?

6. 9.06 + 4.976 = ?

7. 0.286 + 8.76 + 59.6 = ?

8. 4.307 + 99.82 + 62.7 + 3.942 = ?

9.   7.85
    + 29.726

10.   8.37
      34.103
    + 9.2376

11. At the beginning of the fall semester at the Tech College, Dick spent $850.60 for tuition, $287.39 for books, $630.50 for meals, and $785.90 for a room. Find the total cost of Dick's fall semester.

12. Lorraine's checking account balance was $1,650.37 at the beginning of the month. She made the following deposits: $117.10, $23.07, $331.14, and $202.49. What is Lorraine's new balance?

13. A salesman records his daily mileage to be included in his expense report at the end of the week. The following mileages were recorded; 79.3 miles, 114.8 miles, 88.3 miles, 157.8 miles, and 91.6 miles. How many miles did he drive altogether?

Answers to Exercise 3.3

1. 339.167

2. 52.01

3. 259.974

4. $699.96

5. $2,302.93

6. 14.036

7. 68.646

8. 170.769

9. 37.576

10. 51.7106

11. $2,554.39

12. $2,324.17

13. 531.8 miles

3.4 Subtracting Decimal Numbers

Just as in the addition of decimal numbers, we must align the decimal points when we subtract decimal numbers.

Example 1. Subtract: 123.45
                          − 15.7

107.75

$$\begin{array}{r} 123.45 \\ -\ 15.7 \\ \hline 107.75 \end{array}$$

Example 2. Subtract 0.69 − 0.3111

First arrange vertically, with the decimal points aligned. Then subtract.

$$\begin{array}{r} 0.69\,00 \\ -0.3111 \\ \hline 0.3789 \end{array}$$

52

EXERCISE 3.4

Subtract the following decimal numbers. Check your answers using your calculator.

1. $12.34 - 8.09$

   (handwritten)
   $$\begin{array}{r} 12.34 \\ 8.09 \\ \hline 4.25 \end{array}$$

2. $37 - 1.503$

   (handwritten)
   $$\begin{array}{r} 37.000 \\ 1.503 \\ \hline 35.497 \end{array}$$

3. $529.13 - 89.709$

   (handwritten)
   $$\begin{array}{r} 529.130 \\ 89.709 \\ \hline 439.421 \end{array}$$

4. John's temperature reading is 102.7° Fahrenheit. Normal body temperature is 98.6° Fahrenheit. How much above normal is John's temperature?

   (handwritten)
   $$\begin{array}{r} 102.7 \\ 98.6 \\ \hline 4.1 \end{array}$$

5. What is the current value of a stock in Company A, if it was originally purchased at $16.23 per share and the price dropped in value by $.57 per share?

   (handwritten)
   $$\begin{array}{r} 16.23 \\ .57 \\ \hline 15.66 \end{array}$$

6. $72.021 - 8.32 = ?$

7. $27 - 7.64 = ?$

   (handwritten)
   $$\begin{array}{r} 27.00 \\ 7.64 \\ \hline 19.36 \end{array}$$

8. $7.01 - 3.523 = ?$

   (handwritten)
   $$\begin{array}{r} 7.010 \\ 3.523 \\ \hline 3.487 \end{array}$$

9. $\begin{array}{r} 23.410 \\ - \ 0.219 \\ \hline 23.191 \end{array}$

10. $\begin{array}{r} 67.93502 \\ - 53.07035 \\ \hline 14.86467 \end{array}$

    (handwritten, for 11)
    $$\begin{array}{r} 50.00 \\ 31.33 \\ \hline 18.67 \end{array}$$

    (handwritten, for 12)
    $$\begin{array}{r} 429.95 \\ 72.50 \\ \hline 357.45 \end{array}$$

11. How much change would you receive from a $50 bill if you made a purchase of $31.33?

12. If a microwave oven that regularly sells for $429.95 is marked down $72.50, what is the sale price?

Answers to Exercise 3.4

1.	4.25	5.	$15.66	9.	23.191
2.	35.497	6.	63.701	10.	14.86467
3.	439.421	7.	19.36	11.	$18.67
4.	4.1°	8.	3.487	12.	$357.45

3.5 Rounding Off Decimal Numbers

The rule for rounding off decimal numbers is similar to the rule for rounding off whole numbers.

Example 1. Round 0.32 to the nearest tenth.

Step 1: Underline the tenths digit: 0.321

Step 2: Look at the digit immediately to the right (the hundredths digit). This digit is 2, which is less than 5, so the underlined digit is not changed.

Step 3: Discard the digits to the right of the underlined digit: 0.3.

Note that Step 3 is different when rounding off decimal numbers. We discard the digits to the right of the underlined digit, instead of replacing them with zeros. If we expressed our rounded-off number as 0.300, it would be rounded to thousandths, not tenths.

Example 2. Round 5.0632 to the nearest hundredth.

5.0632 ≈ 5.06   The symbol ≈ is read as "approximately equal to"

Example 3. Round 17.6666 to the nearest thousandth.

17.6666 ≈ 17.667

54

One note of caution! In many real-life situations the rule for rounding-off decimals will not apply. If you plan to mail a letter that weighs 1.3 ounces, the post office will charge you for two ounces, not for one ounce. If the price of three cans of soup is $1.00 and you buy only one can, you will pay 34 cents, not 33 cents.

EXERCISE 3.5

1. Round 3.456 to the nearest tenth.   3.5 .010

2. Round 0.00999 to the nearest thousandth.

3. Round 14.5679873 to the nearest millionth.   .567987

4. Round 5.00873 to the nearest hundredth.   .009   .010?

5. Round 2.00500 to the nearest hundredth.   2.01

6. Round 1.849 to the nearest hundredth.   1.85

7. Round 14.049 to the nearest tenth.   14.00

8. Round 0.24687 to the nearest ten-thousandth.   .2469

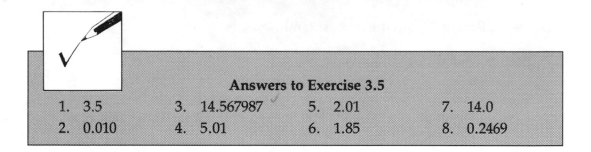

Answers to Exercise 3.5

1. 3.5	3. 14.567987	5. 2.01	7. 14.0
2. 0.010	4. 5.01	6. 1.85	8. 0.2469

3.6 Multiplying Decimal Numbers

It isn't necessary to align decimal points when multiplying decimal numbers. Multiplying decimal numbers is done in the same way as for whole numbers. The number of decimal places in the product is equal to the sum of the decimal places in each factor.

Example 1. Multiply 34.75 × 0.123.

$$
\begin{array}{ll}
34.75 & \text{2 decimal places} \\
\times \quad 0.123 & \text{3 decimal places} \\
\hline
4.27425 & 2 + 3 = 5 \text{ decimal places}
\end{array}
$$

Example 2. Use a calculator to multiply 34.75 × 0.123.

| 34.75 | × | 0.123 | = | 4.27425 |

340
6375
4 0375

EXERCISE 3.6

Multiply the following decimal numbers.

1. 23.17×100 *2317*

2. 3.005×2.06 *6.1903 ≈ 6.2*

3. 89.794×3.72 *334.03368 ≈ 334.00*

4. At the local service station the selling price of regular unleaded gasoline is $1.049 per gallon. If you buy 13.3 gallons of gasoline, how much do you pay?   *13.95 (17.)*

5. The state income tax on your business is $504 plus 0.06 times your profit. If your profit last year was $13,689, what amount of income tax did you owe?   *1325.34*

6. $357 \times 0.31 = ?$ *110.67*

7. $0.0123 \times 1.08 = ?$ *.013284*

8. $41.17 \times 5.6 = ?$ *230.552*

9. If your mortgage payments are $723.50 per month, what is the total amount of the payments for 25 years?   *$217050.00*

10. How many miles would you drive in one five-day work week, if the distance from your home to your work is 19.7 miles? (Consider the distance to and from work.)   *98.5 × 2 = 197*

11. If 3 apples sell for .79 cents, how much will $1\frac{1}{2}$ dozen apples cost?   *4.74*

12. If the annual interest rate for borrowing money was 0.094 times the sum of money borrowed, find the interest on a loan of $4,400 over 3 years.   *413.6 × 3   1240.80*

13. Phillip is paid $8.50 an hour for a 40-hour work week and 1.5 times the regular rate for overtime. How much gross pay would be received for a week in which he worked 45 hours?   *403.75*

14. A piece of television cable sells for 53.7 cents a foot. How much would an 83-foot length of cable cost?   *$44.57*

15. If a new car loses 0.31 of its value during the first year, how much would a $11,370 car be worth at the end of one year?   *3524.7   7845.30*

56

Answers to Exercise 3.6

1. 2317

2. 6.1903

3. 334.03368

4. $13.95

5. $1,325.34

6. 110.67

7. 0.013284

8. 230.552

9. $217,050

10. 197 miles

11. $4.74

12. $1,240.80

13. $403.75

14. $44.57

15. $7,845.30

3.7 Dividing Decimal Numbers

Dividing decimal numbers is almost the same as dividing whole numbers, except that we must first make the divisor a whole number. To do this, we move the decimal point until it is to the right of the last digit in the divisor. Then we must move the decimal point in the dividend the same number of places to the right as we did in the divisor. The decimal point in the quotient is placed directly over the decimal point in the dividend.

Example 1. Divide 1.5328 by 0.13.

Step 1: Make the divisor a whole number.

0.13 ⟶ 13.

We moved the decimal point two places to the right.

Step 2: Adjust the dividend accordingly.

1.5328 ⟶ 153.28

Step 3: Divide, adding zeros to the dividend as necessary. The decimal point in the quotient is directly over the decimal point in the dividend.

$$\frac{11.790769}{13)\,153.280000}\quad \text{or 11.791 rounded to the nearest thousandth.}$$

EXERCISE 3.7

Divide the following decimal numbers. Round off your answers to the nearest hundredth.

1. 15.7 ÷ 2.5

2. 34.409 ÷ 0.47

3. 0.76543 ÷ 100

4. 173.712 ÷ 6.09

5. 1360.997 ÷ 1.1112

6. James received an inheritance of $45,350 from his uncle's estate. If James' inheritance represents 0.7 of his uncle's total estate, what was the total value of the estate?

7. 7.04 ÷ 3.2 = ?

8. 44.4 ÷ 0.06 = ?

9. 0.23401 ÷ 6.9 = ?

10. 0.2307 ÷ 26.7 = ?

11. $1.0478 \div 0.413 = ?$ *2.537046*

12. A retail management trainee earns $21,560.30 for a year's work. How much does she earn in one month?   *1796.70*

13. Gasoline tax is $0.16 per gallon. How many gallons of gasoline were used if $21.34 was paid in taxes?   *133.3*

14. A shopping mall rented 48,862.5 square feet of space for $114,826,875. How much was received for each square foot?   *(2349.00 CALC)*

15. Heating oil sells for $1.69 per gallon. Charles received a bill from the oil company for $401.21. How many gallons of oil were delivered?   *237.4*

16. Which is a better buy: a ½-inch, 40-foot hose costing $7.20, or a ½-inch, 60-foot hose costing $10.49?

Answers to Exercise 3.7

1. 6.28	9. 0.03
2. 73.21	10. 0.01
3. 0.01	11. 2.54
4. 28.52	12. $1,796.69
5. 1224.80	13. 133.38 gal
6. $64,785.71	14. $2,350 per square foot
7. 2.20	15. 237.40 gal
8. 740.00	16. A 60-ft hose costing $10.49

$\frac{3}{4} = \frac{75}{100}$ or 0.75

4.0 PERCENT

$125\% = \frac{125}{100} = 1.25$

A *percent* is a fraction whose denominator is 100. Twenty-five percent, or 25% means 25 parts out of 100. Percents are frequently expressed as decimals. For example, 25 percent can be written as 0.25.

To convert a decimal to a percent, move the decimal point two places to the right and add the percent sign.

Example 1. Convert (a) 0.35, (b) 0.05, and (c) 12.73 to percents.

   (a) 0.35 = 35%

   (b) 0.05 = 5%

   (c) 12.73 = 1273%

To convert a percent to a decimal, drop the percent sign and move the decimal point two places to the left.

Example 2. Convert (a) 35%, (b) 15.5%, and (c) 125% to decimals.

   (a) 35%   = 0.35

   (b) 15.5% = 0.155

   (c) 125% = 1.25

To convert a fraction to a percent, first change the fraction to a decimal, then move the decimal point two places to the right and add the percent sign.

Example 3. Convert (a) $\frac{1}{5}$, (b) $\frac{3}{8}$, and (c) $2\frac{3}{5}$ to percents.

   (a) $\frac{1}{5} = 0.20 = 20\%$

   (b) $\frac{3}{8} = 0.375 = 37.5\%$ 37.5

   (c) $2\frac{3}{5} = \frac{13}{5} = 2.6 = 260\%$ ✓

Note that in (c) we first changed the mixed number to an improper fraction.

To convert a percent to a fraction, drop the percent sign, place the number over 100, and simplify if possible.

60

$130\% = \dfrac{130}{100} = \dfrac{13}{10}$ *(handwritten)*

Example 4. Convert (a) 13%, (b) 50%, (c) 130%, (d) 28.4%, and (e) $16\frac{2}{3}\%$ to fractions and reduce to lowest terms.

(a) $13\% = \dfrac{13}{100}$ ✓

(b) $50\% = \dfrac{50}{100} = \dfrac{1}{2}$ ✓

(c) $130\% = \dfrac{130}{100} = \dfrac{13}{10}$

(d) $28.4\% = \dfrac{28.4}{100} = \dfrac{28.4 \times 10}{100 \times 10} = \dfrac{284}{1000} = \dfrac{71}{250}$

(handwritten) $\neq 28.4\% = \dfrac{284}{100} = \dfrac{284}{1000} = \dfrac{71}{250}$

(e) $16\dfrac{2}{3}\% = \dfrac{16\frac{2}{3}}{100} = \dfrac{\frac{50}{3}}{100} = \dfrac{50}{3} \times \dfrac{1}{100} = \dfrac{50}{300} = \dfrac{1}{6}$ *(handwritten)* $.16$

Note that in (d) we had a numerator that was a decimal. In (e) we had a numerator that was a mixed number. If the numerator of a fraction is a fraction, decimal, or mixed number, we have a *complex fraction*. These complex fractions need to be simplified so that ultimately both the numerator and denominator are whole numbers.

═══════════════════════════════

EXERCISE 4.0

Convert the following decimals to percents.

1. 0.17 *(handwritten)* 17%

2. 111.05 *(handwritten)* 11105%

3. 0.153 *(handwritten)* 15.3%

4. 0.0045 *(handwritten)* .45%

5. 0.88 *(handwritten)* 88%

6. 0.03 *(handwritten)* 3%

7. 0.6 *(handwritten)* 60%

8. 0.31 *(handwritten)* 31%

9. 0.7382 *(handwritten)* 73.82%

10. 0.0554 *(handwritten)* 5.54%

11. 12 *(handwritten)* 1200%

12. 125 *(handwritten)* 12500%

13. 5 *(handwritten)* 500%

14. 93.2 *(handwritten)* 9320%

15. 12.7 *(handwritten)* 1270%

16. 45.67 *(handwritten)* 4567%

17. 0.20 *(handwritten)* 20%

18. 0.02 *(handwritten)* 2%

19. 0.66 *(handwritten)* 66%

20. 0.99 *(handwritten)* 99%

Convert the following percents to decimals.

21. 110% ~~1.1~~   28. 150% 1.5

22. 93% ~~.93~~   29. 6.5% .065

23. 213.3% 2.133   30. 16.4% .164

24. 0.0025% .000025   31. 3.09% .039

25. 25% .25   32. 0.45% .0045

26. 83% .83   33. 0.007% .00007

27. 425% 4.25   34. 101% 1.01

Convert the following fractions to percents.

35. $\dfrac{1}{8}$ 12.5%

36. $\dfrac{9}{5}$ 180%

37. $\dfrac{3}{32}$ 9.37%

38. $\dfrac{537}{1000}$ 53.7% $\dfrac{12\frac{5}{}}{100}$ $\dfrac{12.5}{100}$ $\dfrac{12\frac{5}{10}}{100}$ $\dfrac{\frac{125}{10}}{100}$

Convert the following percents to fractions and simplify.

39. 12.5% $12\frac{5}{100}$ $\dfrac{12.05}{100}$ $\dfrac{241}{20}$ $12\frac{1}{2}$ $\frac{1}{8}$ 47. $5\dfrac{3}{4}$% $\dfrac{\frac{23}{4}}{100} = \dfrac{23}{4} \times \dfrac{1}{100} = \dfrac{23}{400}$

40. 81.65% $\dfrac{1\frac{25}{100}}{50}$

41. 44.88% $44\frac{88}{100}$ $\frac{22}{25}$ $\dfrac{44\frac{88}{100}}{100}$ $\dfrac{44.88 \times}{100}$ 48. $8\dfrac{2}{3}$% $\dfrac{25}{3} \times \dfrac{1}{100}$ $\dfrac{1}{12}$ $\dfrac{25}{300}$ $\frac{1}{12}$

42. 400.1%   49. 37.5%

43. $5\dfrac{3}{4}$% $\dfrac{\frac{23}{4}}{100} \times \dfrac{1}{100}$ $\dfrac{23}{400}$ ✓   50. $\dfrac{1}{8}$% $\dfrac{\frac{1}{8}}{100} = \dfrac{1}{8} \times \dfrac{1}{100} = \dfrac{1}{800}$

44. $16\dfrac{2}{3}$%   51. $\dfrac{2}{3}$% $\dfrac{\frac{2}{3}}{100}$ $\dfrac{2}{3} \times \dfrac{1}{100}$ $\dfrac{2}{300}$ $\dfrac{1}{150}$

45. 120% $\frac{2}{5}$ ✓   52. 205%

46. $11\dfrac{1}{9}$% $\dfrac{\frac{100}{9} \times \frac{1}{100}}{}$ $\dfrac{100}{900} = \dfrac{1}{9}$ 53. 700%

62

Answers to Exercise 4.0

1. 17%

2. 11,105%

3. 15.3%

4. 0.45%

5. 88%

6. 3%

7. 60%

8. 31%

9. 73.82%

10. 5.54%

11. 1200%

12. 12,500%

13. 500%

14. 9320%

15. 1270%

16. 4567%

17. 20%

18. 2%

19. 66%

20. 99%

21. 1.10

22. 0.93

23. 2.133

24. 0.000025

25. 0.25

26. 0.83

27. 4.25

28. 1.5

29. 0.065

30. 0.164

31. 0.0309

32. 0.0045

33. 0.00007

34. 1.01

35. 12.5%

36. 180%

37. 9.375%

38. 53.7%

39. $\frac{1}{8}$

40. $\frac{1633}{2000}$

41. $\frac{561}{1250}$

42. $\frac{4001}{1000}$ or $4\frac{1}{1000}$

43. $\frac{23}{400}$

44. $\frac{1}{6}$

45. $\frac{6}{5}$ or $1\frac{1}{5}$

46. $\frac{1}{9}$

47. $\frac{23}{400}$

48. $\frac{13}{150}$

49. $\frac{3}{8}$

50. $\frac{1}{800}$

51. $\frac{1}{150}$

52. $2\frac{1}{20}$

53. 7

P A R T

II

Applications

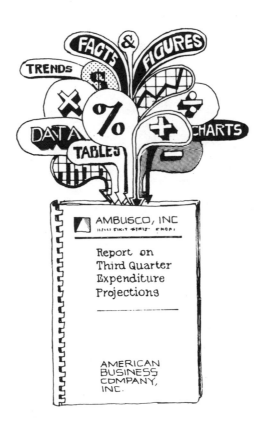

EQUATION
5 RULES

1. You can add the same no to both
sides of
an equation

2. You can subtract the same no from
both sides

3. Both sides of an equation can
be multiplied by the same no
(NOT A ZERO No)

4. Both sides of an equation can
be multiplied by the same (NON ZERO)
Number.

4. Both sides of an equation can
be divided by the same NON-ZERO
Number

5. When an equation contains
Parenthesis we use the distributive
law of multiplication before solving
for the unknown. The Distributive
law of multiplication states that

$$a(b+c) = ab + ac$$

5.0 EQUATIONS

An *equation* is a statement that two mathematical expressions are equal. For example, $3 + 5 = 8$ and $x + 7 = 11$ are equations. In the second example, x is called a *variable* or an unknown, and 7 and 11 are called *constants*. You do not need to know much mathematics to guess that x has to have a value such that adding x to 7 will give 11. That is, $x = 4$.

Example 1.

Solve $3x + 1 = 13$.   ?

If $x = 2$, then $3 \times 2 + 1 = 13$

                                        ?
                              $6 + 1 = 13$
                              $7 \neq 13$ (That is, 7 does not equal 13.)

Therefore $x \neq 2$.

If $x = 4$, then $3 \times 4 + 1 = 13$
                    $12 + 1 = 13$
                    $13 = 13$

(handwritten):
$3x + 1 = 13$
if $x = 4$
$3 \times 4 + 1 = 13$
$13 = 13$
$x = 4$

But guessing is not an efficient way to solve equations. We need a set of rules to solve equations without guessing. To *solve* an equation means to find the value of the variable that will make the equation a true statement.

We have solved the equation. The solution of the equation is $x = 4$.

There are five basic rules we need to know in order to solve an equation.

Rule 1. The same number may be added to both sides of an equation.

a) $3 + 8 = 11$ $3 + 8 + 2 = 11 + 2$ $13 = 13$
b) $x - 2 = 5$ $x - 2 + 2 = 5 + 2$ $x = 7$

Rule 2. The same number may be subtracted from both sides of an equation.

a) $3 + 8 = 11$ $3 + 8 - 3 = 11 - 3$ $8 = 8$
b) $x + 7 = 10$ $x + 7 - 7 = 10 - 7$ $x = 3$

Rule 3. Both sides of an equation may be multiplied by the same non-zero number.

a) $3 + 8 = 11$

$2 \times (3 + 8) = 2 \times 11$

$2 \times 3 + 2 \times 8 = 22$

$6 + 16 = 22$

$22 = 22$

b) $\dfrac{x}{3} = 7$

$3 \times \dfrac{x}{3} = 3 \times 7$

$x = 21$

Rule 4. Both sides of an equation may be divided by the same nonzero number. Remember that you can never divide by zero!

a) $2 \times 5 = 10$

$\dfrac{2 \times 5}{2} = \dfrac{10}{2}$

$5 = \dfrac{10}{2}$

$5 = 5$

b) $6x = 54$

$\dfrac{6x}{6} = \dfrac{54}{6}$

$x = \dfrac{54}{6}$

$x = 9$

Rule 5 When an equation contains parentheses, we use the Distributive Law of Multiplication to remove the parentheses before solving for the unknown. The Distributive Law of Multiplication states that

$a(b + c) = ab + ac$

Example 2. Use the Distributive Law to remove the parentheses from
$3(2x + 6) = 20.$ $6x + 18 = 20$

$3(2x + 6) = 20$

$3(2x) + 3(6) = 20$

$6x + 18 = 20$

Sometimes several of the rules may have to be used to solve an equation. When we solve an equation we wish to *isolate* the variable. That is, we want to get the unknown alone on one side of the equation.

Example 3. Solve $3x - 4 = 17$.

$$3x - 4 = 17$$

Add 4 to each side (Rule 1):

$$3x - 4 + 4 = 17 + 4$$

Divide both sides by 3 (Rule 4):

$$3x = 21$$
$$\frac{3x}{3} = \frac{21}{3}$$
$$x = 7$$

Handwritten:
$$3x - 4 = 17$$
$$3x - 4 + 4 = 17 + 4$$
$$3x = 21$$
$$\frac{3x}{3} = \frac{21}{3}$$
$$x = 7$$

Let's check our solution to see if the value $x = 7$ satisfies the original equation.

Replace x with 7:

$$3x - 4 = 17$$
$$3(7) - 4 = 17$$
$$21 - 4 = 17$$
$$17 = 17 \quad \text{It checks!}$$

Handwritten:
$$3x - 4 = 17$$
$$3(7)4 = 17$$
$$21 - 4 = 17$$
$$17 = 17$$

Example 4. Solve $28 + T = 39$.

$$28 + T = 39$$

Subtract 28 from each side (Rule 2):

$$28 - 28 + T = 39 - 28$$
$$T = 11$$

Handwritten: $T = 11$

Example 5. Solve $\frac{1}{2}y - 6 = 8$.

$$\frac{1}{2}y - 6 = 8 \qquad \text{(handwritten: } \tfrac{1}{2}y = 14\text{)}$$

Add 6 to each side (Rule 1):

$$\frac{1}{2}y - 6 + 6 = 8 + 6$$
$$\frac{1}{2}y = 14$$

Multiply both sides by 2 (Rule 3):

$$2\left(\frac{1}{2}y\right) = 2(14) \qquad \text{(handwritten: } y = 28\text{)}$$
$$y = 28$$

Example 6. Solve $w - \frac{2}{3} = \frac{4}{7}$.

$$w - \frac{2}{3} = \frac{4}{7}$$

Add $\frac{2}{3}$ to both sides (Rule 1):

$$w - \frac{2}{3} + \frac{2}{3} = \frac{4}{7} + \frac{2}{3}$$

$$w = \frac{4}{7} + \frac{2}{3} \quad \begin{array}{l}\text{The LCD for the unlike}\\ \text{fractions is 21, so}\end{array}$$

$$w = \frac{12 + 14}{21}$$

$$w = \frac{26}{21} \text{ or } 1\frac{5}{21} \qquad \checkmark$$

Alternative solution to example 6.

Solve $\left(W - \dfrac{2}{3}\right) = \left(\dfrac{4}{7}\right)$

$21(W - \dfrac{2}{3}) = 21(\dfrac{4}{7})$

$21W - 21(\dfrac{2}{3}) = 21(\dfrac{4}{7})$.

$21W - 14 = 12$

$21W = 12 + 14$ Rule 1. (The addition rule)

$21W = 26$

$W = \dfrac{26}{21}$ Rule 4. (the division rule)

1. Find the LCD for 3 and 7. LCD = 21.

2. Multiply both sides of the equation by 21, to remove the fractions.

3. Use the Distributive Law on the left side.

[handwritten:]
$8(2y + 4) = 112$
$16y + 32 = 112$
$16y \; {}^{-32} = 80$
$\dfrac{16}{16} \qquad = \dfrac{80}{16}$
$y = 5$

[handwritten left margin:]
$10x + 7 = 3x + 49$
$10x + 7 - 7 = 3x + 49 - 7$
$10x = 3x + 42$
$7x = 42$
$\div 7$
$x = 6$

Example 7. Solve $10x + 7 = 3x + 49$.

$10x + 7 = 3x + 49$

Subtract 7 from each side (Rule 2):

$10x + 7 - 7 = 3x + 49 - 7$

$10x = 3x + 42$

Subtract $3x$ from both sides (Rule 2):

$10x - 3x = 3x - 3x + 42$

$7x = 42$

Divide both sides by 7 (Rule 4):

$\dfrac{7x}{7} = \dfrac{42}{7}$

$x = 6$

Example 8. Solve $8(2y + 4) = 112$.

$8(2y + 4) = 112$

Remove the parentheses using the Distributive Law (Rule 5):

$8(2y) + 8(4) = 112$

$16y + 32 = 112$

Subtract 32 from both sides (Rule 2):

$16y + 32 - 32 = 112 - 32$

$16y = 80$

Divide both sides by 16 (Rule 4):

$y = 5$

Example 9. Solve 61.393 = 8.41b.

$$61.393 = 8.41b$$

Divide both sides by 8.41 (Rule 4):

$$\frac{61.393}{8.41} = \frac{8.41b}{8.41}$$

$$7.3 = b$$

That is, $b = 7.3$

Handwritten:
$61.393 = 8.41b$
$7.3 = b$
$10p + 7 = 56 + 3p$
$10p - 3p + 7 = 56 + 3p - 3p$
$7p + 7 = 56$
$\frac{p+1}{7} = 8$

$10p + 7 = 56 + 3p$
$10p = 48 + 3p$
$7p = 49 + 0p$
$7p = \frac{49}{7} =$
$p = 7$

EXERCISE 5.0

Solve each of the following equations.

1. $12y + 6 = 30$ *(handwritten: $12y + 6 = 30$, $12y = 24$, $y = 2$)*

2. $\dfrac{x}{12} - 15 = 38$ *(handwritten: $\frac{x}{12} - 15 = 38 + 15$, $\frac{x}{12} = \frac{53}{1}$, 636)*

3. $56.78 = y - 13.4$ *(handwritten: $y = 70.18$)*

4. $6x + 4(x + 7) = 148$ *(handwritten: $6x + 4x + 28 = 148$, $10x = 120$, $\frac{120}{10} = 12$)*

5. $\dfrac{x - 5}{1.3} = 42.5$ *(handwritten: 55.25, $x = 60.25$)*

6. $4y = 20$ *(handwritten: = 5)*

7. $3x + 4 = 13$ *(handwritten: $3x = 9$, $x = 3$)*

8. $10p + 7 = 56 + 3p$

9. $\dfrac{3}{5}w = 9$

10. $5x = \dfrac{2}{3}$

11. $2.31z = 122.199$ *(handwritten: 119.889, 52.9, or 119.890)*

12. $4y - \dfrac{2}{5} = 2\dfrac{2}{5}$ *(handwritten: $2\frac{2}{5} \div 4$)*

13. $x - \dfrac{4}{3} = \dfrac{1}{2}$ *(handwritten: $x = 1\frac{5}{6}$)*

14. $m - 3\dfrac{1}{4} = 2\dfrac{1}{2}$

15. $\left(3\dfrac{1}{3}\right)x = 2\dfrac{1}{4}$

16. $\dfrac{y - 5}{2} = \dfrac{1}{3}$

17. $4(3 - 7x) = -11$

18. $(4y - 3) + y = y + (5 - y)$

19. $3x + \dfrac{3}{2}x - 6 = 114$

20. $\dfrac{2}{5}x + 3 = 4\left(\dfrac{7}{8} + \dfrac{1x}{12}\right)$

21. $0.38 + 1.1z = 0.6$

22. $\dfrac{0.4}{0.014} = \dfrac{0.08}{x}$

23. $4.3 = 0.3y - 7.34$

24. $\dfrac{4}{5}x = \dfrac{1}{10}x + \dfrac{2}{5}$

25. $\dfrac{3}{4}x = \dfrac{1}{3}$

Handwritten at bottom: $\dfrac{\frac{5}{4} + \frac{13}{4}}{4}$ $\dfrac{10 + 13}{4}$ $\dfrac{23}{4}$ $5\frac{3}{4}$ or $\dfrac{23}{4}$ M

Answers to Exercise 5.0

1. $y = 2$

2. $x = 636$

3. $y = 70.18$

4. $x = 12$

5. $x = 60.25$

6. $y = 5$

7. $x = 3$

8. $p = 7$

9. $w = 15$

10. $x = \dfrac{2}{15}$ ✓

11. $z = 52.9$

12. $y = \dfrac{3}{5}$

13. $x = \dfrac{11}{6}$

14. $m = 5\dfrac{3}{4}$ ✓

15. $x = \dfrac{27}{40}$

16. $y = \dfrac{17}{3}$ or $5\dfrac{2}{3}$

17. $x = \dfrac{23}{28}$

18. $y = \dfrac{8}{5}$ or $1\dfrac{3}{5}$

19. $x = \dfrac{80}{3}$ or $26\dfrac{2}{3}$

20. $x = \dfrac{15}{2}$ or $7\dfrac{1}{2}$

21. $z = 0.2$

22. $x = 0.0028$

23. $y = 38.8$

24. $x = \dfrac{4}{7}$

25. $x = \dfrac{4}{9}$

6.0 FORMULAS

Webster's dictionary defines the word *formula* as ''a set of algebraic symbols expressing a mathematical fact, principle, rule, etc. such as $I = PRT$.'' Many problems in business and in other areas involve the use of formulas. A formula is really an equation in which all the terms are represented by letters. If we know the values of all the terms except one, we can substitute those values for the letters of the formula. We can then solve the resulting equation.

Example 1. Given $I = PRT$. If $P = 4{,}000$, $R = 0.12$, and $T = 2$, find I.

$$I = PRT$$

Substitute the values of P, R, and T:

$$I = 4{,}000 \times 0.12 \times 2 \qquad = 960$$

When using formulas, you will need to meet two objectives. First, you must be able to evaluate formulas by substituting numbers for variables. Second, you must be able to solve a formula for a specific variable. Some examples of formulas are:

$I = PRT$	Interest = principal × rate × time
$D = RT$	Distance = rate × time
$A = R \times B$	Amount of the base = rate × base
$S = P + PRT$	The amount to which a given principal will accumulate = principal plus principal × interest rate × time
$A = \frac{1}{2}bh$	Area of a triangle = one-half the length of the base × the length of the altitude.

There are as many different ways of writing a formula as there are letters in the formula.

Example 2. Write the formula $I = PRT$ four different ways (since the formula contains four letters).

(1) $I = PRT$

Divide both sides by PT.

(2) $\dfrac{I}{PT} = R$

Divide both sides of equation (1) by RT.

(3) $\dfrac{I}{RT} = P$

Divide both sides of equation (1) by PR.

(4) $\dfrac{I}{PR} = T$

Example 3. Write the formula $C = 25R$ to express R in terms of C.

$C = 25R$

Divide both sides of the formula by 25:

$$\frac{C}{25} = \frac{25R}{25} \qquad\qquad \frac{C}{25} = R \qquad\qquad R = \frac{C}{25}$$

Example 4. Given $ax + b = c$; $a \neq 0$. Express x in terms of a, b, and c.

$ax + b = c$

$ax + b - b = c - b$

$ax = c - b$

$x = \dfrac{c - b}{a}$

Example 5. Given $I = PRT$; $I = \$540$; $R = 0.045$; and $P = \$6,000$. Find T.

$I = PRT$

Divide both sides by PR: $\dfrac{I}{PR} = T$

That is, $T = \dfrac{I}{PR}$

Substitute the values of I, P, and R.

$$T = \frac{540}{(6000)(0.045)}$$

$$= \frac{540}{270} \qquad = 2 \text{ (years)}$$

540	÷	(	6000	×	0.045	)	=	2

EXERCISE 6.0

1. Solve $2x + y = 6$ for y.   2. Solve $A = P + PRT$ for T.

In each formula, substitute the given values and find the value of the unknown variable:

3. $D = RT$; $R = 55$ mph, $T = 3.5$ hours

4. $S = (1 + R) C$; $S = \$174$, $R = 45\%$

5. $P = \dfrac{L + I}{T}$, $L = \$800$, $R = 12.4\%$, $T = 2$. Where $I = PRT$

   $Monthly\ payment = \dfrac{\text{loan amount} + \text{interest}}{\text{number of months}}$

6. Solve $P = BR$ for B.   8. Solve $P = 2l + 2w$ for w.

7. Solve $I = PRT$ for T.   9. Solve $A = \dfrac{1}{2}bh$ for h.

10. Solve $C = 5x + 1000$ for x.

11. Solve $E = \dfrac{Y + P}{Y}$ for P.

12. Solve $y = mxt + b$ for m.

13. Solve $A = P(1 + NI)$ for N.

14. Solve $\dfrac{T_1}{T_2} = \dfrac{V_1}{V_2}$ for V_2.

15. Solve $A = M - K$ for K.

16. $I = PRT$; $P = \$9,000$, $R = 4.5\%$, $T = 2$ yr. Find I.

17. $I = PRT$; $I = \$582.97$, $P = \$15,756$, $T = 1$ yr. Find R.

18. $y = mx + b$; $y = 35$, $x = 4$, $b = 3$. Find m.

19. $G = MP$; $M = 11,110$, $P = \$3.15$. Find G.

20. $c = 3x + 800$; $x = 155$. Find c.

21. $A = P + I$; $A = \$15,500$, $I = \$3,600$. Find P.

22. $C = \dfrac{300D + 7M}{100}$; $D = 14$, $M = 650$. Find C.

23. $C = \dfrac{300D + 7M}{100}$; $C = \$76.25$, $M = 875$. Find D.

24. $V = C(1 - RT)$; $C = \$560$, $T = 6$ yr. $R = 5\%$. Find V.

25. $A = P(1 + RT)$; $P = \$14,600$, $R = 6.5\%$, $T = 6$ months. Find A.
    (Hint: Express T in terms of years.)

26. $A = P(1 + RT)$; $A = \$177,370.83$, $P = \$171,580$, $T = 9$ months. Find R.

Answers to Exercise 6.0

1. $2x + y = 6$
   $y = 6 - 2x$

2. $A = P + PRT$
   $A - P = PRT$
   $\dfrac{A - P}{PR} = T$

3. $D = RT$
   $D = (55\text{ mph})(3.5\text{ hrs.})$
   $D = 192.5\text{ miles}$

4. $S = (1 + R)\,C$
   $\$174 = (1 + 0.45)\,C$
   $\$174 = (1.45)\,C$
   $\$120 = C$

5. $P = \dfrac{L + I}{T}$
   $P = \dfrac{\$800 + 800(2)(.124)}{2}$
   $P = \dfrac{800 + 198.4}{2}$
   $P = \dfrac{998.4}{2}$
   $P = \$499.20$

6. $B = \dfrac{P}{R}$

7. $T = \dfrac{I}{PR}$

8. $w = \dfrac{P - 2l}{2}$

9. $h = \dfrac{2A}{b}$

10. $x = \dfrac{C - 1000}{5}$

11. $P = EY - Y$

12. $m = \dfrac{y - b}{xt}$

13. $N = \dfrac{A - P}{PI}$

14. $V_2 = \dfrac{V_1 T_2}{T_1}$

15. $K = M - A$

16. $810

17. 3.7%

18. 8

19. $34,996.50

20. 1,265

21. $11,900

22. 87.50

23. 5

24. $392

25. $15074.50

26. 4.5%

7.0   THE PERCENTAGE FORMULA

One of the most useful formulas in business is the percentage formula: $P = RB$, where P equals a percentage of the base, B, and R equals the rate (or percent). Recall that if any two of the three variables are known, then the value of the remaining variable can be found.

Students often have difficulty determining which is the P, R, or B. Here is a simple way to figure it out: R is always given as a percent; B is always the number that follows the word *of*; and P is what remains—P can also be thought of as coming before the word *is*.

For example, 10 percent of 40 is 4. Here, R is 10 (it comes before the word *percent*) B is 40 (it comes after the word *of*), and P is 4 (it comes after the word *is*).

Example 1. Identify R, B, and P:

    (a)   40 is what percent of 320?
           ↑   ↑   ↑
           P R B

    (c)   What is 75% of 200?
           ↑   ↑   ↑
           P R B

    (b)   10 is 8% of what number?
           ↑   ↑   ↑
           P R B

7.1 Solving Problems with the Percentage Formula

The basic percentage formula can be discussed from two perspectives: with a visual geometric approach using a circle (see Figure 7.1) and with proportions.

Since the formula $P = R \times B$ has three variables, if we know any two of them we can find the remaining one.

The circle shown in Figure 7.1 may help you solve the percentage formula more easily. P is always in the half-circle. To find P, B, or R, simply shade the unknown segment you are solving for. If the remaining variables are horizontal, multiply them; if they are vertical, divide them.

Figure 7.1 The $P = RB$ circle

Horizontal: multiply.
$P = R \times B$

Vertical: divide.
$R = \dfrac{P}{B}$

Example 2. Given R and B, find P.

Example 3. Given P and B, find R.

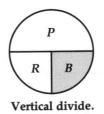

Vertical divide.

$$B = \frac{P}{R}$$

Example 4. Given P and R, find B.

Once you know which form of the formula to use, you can substitute the given values for two of the terms to find the third, unknown term.

Example 5. What is 14% of 75.3? ✓

$$P = RB$$
$$= (0.14)(75.3)$$
$$= 10.542$$

Example 6. 10.542 is what percent of 75.3?

$$R = \frac{P}{B}$$
$$= \frac{10.542}{75.3}$$
$$= 0.14 \qquad 14\%$$
$$= 14\%$$

Example 7. 10.542 is 14% of what amount?

$$B = \frac{P}{R}$$
$$= \frac{10.542}{0.14}$$
$$= 75.3$$

Example 8. Use a calculator to find 32.08% of 101.

$$P = RB$$
$$= (0.3208)(101)$$

Multiply using a calculator: | 0.3208 | | × | | 101 | | = | *32.4008*

or | 101 | | × | | 32.08 | | = | | 2nd | | = | *32.4008*

or | 32.08% | | 2nd | | = | | × | | 101 | | = | *32.4008*

NOTE: The key sequence may be different for your calculator. Refer to your manual.

The second method we can use in working with the percentage formula is the proportion method. Before we use proportions, we need to understand what a ratio is. A *ratio* is a comparison of two quantities. A ratio is simply a fraction. Earlier in this text when we studied fractions, we could have called our fractions ratios. Thus $\frac{1}{2}$, $\frac{7}{3}$, and $\frac{4}{5}$ are ratios.

A *proportion* is a comparison of ratios. For example, $\frac{1}{2}=\frac{5}{10}$ is a proportion. Since a proportion is also an equation, the rules for solving equations apply. Of all of the different mathematical concepts you will encounter in your study of mathematics, the concepts of ratio and proportion have perhaps the greatest number of everyday practical applications. Proportions are used in mixing ingredients, in comparison shopping, in solving problems using $P = R \times B$, and in many other applications.

We will now use proportions to solve problems based on the $R = RB$ formula. In using proportions, we always need to compare two ratios. The first ratio, the percent ratio, is $\frac{R}{100}$. The second ratio is $\frac{P}{B}$. The proportion is: $\frac{R}{100}=\frac{P}{B}$ or $\frac{\text{Percent}}{100}=\frac{\text{Amount}}{\text{Base}}$

Example 9. 49 is what percent of 102?

$$\frac{R}{100}=\frac{P}{B}$$

Substitute the given values (the amount, P, and the base, B).

$$\frac{R}{100}=\frac{49}{102}$$

$$R=\frac{49\times100}{102}$$

$$=\frac{4900}{102} \text{ or } 48.04\%$$

Example 10. 16 is 80% of what number?

$$\frac{R}{100}=\frac{P}{B}$$

Substitute the values of R and P.

$$\frac{80}{100}=\frac{16}{B}$$

$$80B=16\times100$$

$$B=\frac{1600}{80}=20$$

Example 11. What is 1.06% of 500?

P is the unknown.

Substitute the values of R and B.

$$\frac{1.06}{100}=\frac{P}{500}$$

$$\frac{1.06\times500}{100}=P$$

$$\frac{530}{100}=P$$

$$5.3=P$$

Exercise 7.1

1. 49 is what percent of 102?

2. 312.65 is what percent of 313.46?

3. 16 is 80% of what number?

4. 1.9 is 25% of what number?

5. What is 1.06% of 500?

6. What is 125.4% of 36?

7. What is 54% of 25?

8. What is 0.25% of 2000?

9. What is 1½% of 250?

10. What is 0.075% of 875?

11. 80% of 16.25 is what?

12. 210% of 12 is what?

13. Find 55% of 300.

14. Find 9.7% of 575.

15. Find 31.187% of 97,580.

16. 0.05% of 160 is what?

17. What percent of 75 is 20?

18. What percent of 400 is 12?

19. What percent of 6 is 9?

20. 0.3 is what percent of 50?

21. 45 is what percent of 200?

22. 5 is what percent of 1000?

23. 3.7 is what percent of 135?

24. What percent of 40 is 1?

25. What percent of 11 is 99?

26. 31.97 is what percent of 88.5?

27. 8 is 32% of what?

28. 27 is 27% of what?

29. 87.5 is 76% of what?

30. 0.7% of what is 0.65?

31. 125% of what is 48?

32. 30% of what is 2.7?

33. 66⅔% of what is 9?

34. 200% of what is 3?

35. 5.19% of what is 103.8?

36. 444 is 22.2% of what?

37. You can purchase a computer today for $4,500, which is 35% of the cost three years ago. What was the cost of the computer three years ago? Express your answer to the nearest whole dollar.

38. A new car costs $10,250. Its value depreciates 23% the first year. What is the car's value at the end of the first year?

78

Answers to Exercise 7.1

1. $P = RB$

   $49 = R\,(102)$

   $\dfrac{49}{102} = R$

   $48.04\% = R$

2. $\dfrac{312.65}{313.46} = R$

   $99.74\% = R$

3. $16 = .80B$

   $\dfrac{16}{.80} = B$

   $20 = B$

4. $1.9 = .25B$

   $\dfrac{1.9}{.25} = B$

   $7.6 = B$

5. $P = 0.0106\,(500) = 5.3$

6. $P = 1.254\,(36) = 45.144$

7. 13.5

8. 5

9. 3.75

10. 0.65625

11. 13

12. 25.2

13. 165

14. 55.775

15. 30432.2746

16. 0.08

17. 26.7%

18. 3%

19. 150%

20. 0.6%

21. 22.5%

22. 0.5%

23. 2.74%

24. 2.5%

25. 900%

26. 36.1%

27. 25

28. 100

29. 115.13

30. 92.86

31. 38.4

32. 9

33. 13.50

34. 1.5

35. 2000

36. 2000

37. $12,857

38. $7,892.50

7.2 Commissions

A person's compensation is often paid on a commission basis, particularly if the job involves selling. A commission is a percentage of the total amount of sales. To find the commission earned, we multiply the amount of sales by the *rate of commission*, which is a percent of the sales.

Commission = Rate of commission × Amount of sale

$$C = R \times A$$

Notice how the above formula is just like $P = RB$, but using different letters.

Example 1. Lorraine sells real estate and receives a commission of 5% of the sales price. What is Lorraine's commission on a house that sells for $125,700?

$$C = R \times A$$
$$= (0.05) \times (\$125,700)$$
$$= \$6,285$$

Example 2. Stephen works on a straight commission basis of 4% of his net sales. If Stephen's commission for last week was $205, what was the amount of his net sales?

$$C = R \times A$$
$$205 = 0.04 . A$$
$$\frac{205}{0.04} = A$$
$$\$5,125 = A$$

Example 3. Kim works at Friendly's Restaurant Equipment Company and receives a commission of 1% on the first $1,000 of sales, 1.75% for the next $200 in sales, and 2.1% for all sales over $1,200.

If Kim's total net sales amounted to $2,600, what was her commission?

$$C = R \times A$$
$$= (0.01)(\$1,000) + (0.0175)(\$200) + (0.021)(\$1,400)$$
$$= \$10 + \$3.50 + 29.40$$
$$= \$42.90$$

EXERCISE 7.2

1. John sells textbooks for a total of $53,720. The publisher pays him an 11% commission on his sales. What was the amount of John's commission?

2. Elizabeth's income is based on a fixed salary of $600 per week plus a commission of 5% of her sales. If her sales last week totaled $2,108, what was her income before taxes?

3. A computer salesperson received a commission of $3,607.40 on sales of $47,533. What is the rate of commission?

4. ACE Realty sold a house for $235,000. The firm's commission is 6% of the sales price. What was ACE Realty's commission?

5. A salesperson has a commission rate of 4.7%. What volume of sales must she achieve to earn a commission of $280?

6. David sells skis on a commission of 7.3% of net sales. What is David's commission on net sales of $8,140?

7. Joey is paid a straight commission of 6% on net sales. Last month her gross sales totaled $13,875, with returns totaling $2,124. What was Joey's commission?

8. Robert is a textbook salesman who received a bonus of $1,290 on his yearly sales. If his commission rate is 5% of his total yearly sales, what were his yearly sales?

9. Amy Hanson sells futon mattresses and is paid on a graduated commission basis defined as follows: 4% after the first $3,000 in net sales, $6\frac{1}{2}$% on the next $2,000 in net sales, and $7\frac{1}{4}$% on all net sales over $5,000. If Amy had net sales of $8,175 last month, what was her commission?

10. Mark sells advertising space in a local magazine under a compensation plan of salary plus commission of 3.5% on net sales. Mark's salary is $185 and his net sales last week were $1,592. What was his income last week?

11. Betty receives a monthly salary of $5,500 and a commission of 2% on net sales over $12,500. If last month's sales totaled $17,583, what was her income for the month?

12. The Portsmouth Collection Agency provides a service for local businesses by collecting on delinquent accounts. An agent for the Portsmouth Collection Agency, Michele Croteau, collected $3,780. She was reimbursed at a rate of 25% for her services. She also received $41 for her expenses. After paying Michele's commission and expenses, how much did the Portsmouth Collection Agency receive?

13. If $150 was charged for selling $6,000 worth of goods, what was the rate of commission?

14. The Century 35 Real Estate Agency's fee was $2,361.90. If the rate of commission was $6\frac{3}{4}$%, what was the selling price of the lot that the agency sold?

15. Richard received a $3,570 commission on sales of $42,750. What is Richard's rate of commission?

16. In December, John Croteau submitted orders totaling $21,538, with cancellations amounting to $3,675. John is paid on a graduated commission of 4.5% on the first $8,000 in net sales, 5.5% on the next $4,000, and 6.25% of net sales in excess of $12,000. What were John's earnings?

82

Answers to Exercise 7.2

1. $C = \$53{,}720 \times 11\% = \$5{,}909.20$

2. $I = \$600 + 0.05\,(\$2{,}108) = \$705.40$

3. $\$3{,}670.40 = R \times (\$47{,}533);\ R = 7.6\%$

4. $C = .06\,(\$235{,}000) = \$14{,}100$

5. $5{,}957.45

6. $594.22

7. $705.06

8. $25,800

9. $480.19

10. $240.72

11. $5601.66

12. $2,794

13. 2.5%

14. $34.991.11

15. 8.35%

16. $946.44

7.3 Percent Increase (Mark-up)

We encounter the concept of *percent increase* whenever a person is given a pay raise, the value of a house appreciates, the price of gasoline goes up, or the property tax on a home is raised.

The amount of increase is equal to the rate of increase multiplied by the original amount. In other words, it is once again $P = R \times B$.

Example 1. The price of gasoline last year was $1.09 per gallon. There has been a 40% increase in the price. What is the amount of increase?

$$\text{Amount of increase} = \text{Rate of increase} \times \text{Original amount}$$
$$= 0.40 \times \$1.09$$
$$= \$.44 \text{ or } 44 \text{ cents}$$

44 cents
$1.53

Occasionally, we know the original amount and the new amount and wish to find the rate of increase.

Example 2. Last year the price of gasoline was $1.09 per gallon. Today it is $1.53 per gallon. What is the rate of increase?

for Rate of increase READ MARGIN in UK & USA

$$\text{Rate of Increase} = \frac{\text{Amount of increase}}{\text{Original amount}}$$
$$= \frac{\$.44}{\$1.09}$$
$$= 0.4036 \text{ or approximately } 40\%$$

40% margin

Example 3. The cost of a man's three-piece suit is $350. The cost will increase by 12% in January. What will be the new purchase price of the suit?

First, we need to determine the amount of increase.

$$P = R \times B$$
$$= .12 \times \$350$$
$$= \$42$$

Then we must add this amount of increase to the original amount.

$$\text{New purchase price} = \$350 + \$42$$
$$= \$392$$

EXERCISE 7.3

1. The ABC Computer Company hired 250 new employees between July and December. At the beginning of the year, the total number of employees was 2,000. What was the percent increase in the number of employees?

2. Last month the total sales for the printing company was $25,000. This month's total sales were $37,500. What was the percent increase?

3. After the Christmas holiday season Sam's weight increased from 167 lbs. to 183 lbs. What is the percent increase in Sam's weight?

4. A college bookstore buys a used book from a student for $11.50 and resells it for $20.75. What was the percent of gain, based on the cost to the bookstore?

5. A share of common stock rose from $27\frac{1}{2}$ per share to $29\frac{5}{8}$ per share. Find the percent change in the stock value.

6. A salesperson's salary increased by 7%. If the previous salary was $17,000 per year, what is the salesperson's new salary?

7. Deborah has $737 in her savings account. She makes a deposit of $53. What is the percent increase in her account?

8. A floor lamp costs $155.50 and the mark-up rate is 40%. Find (a) the mark-up and (b) the selling price.

9. A coffee table that costs $119.22 sells for $160.95. Find (a) the mark-up and (b) the rate of mark-up.

10. The JM Department Store sells a bottle of perfume at $125 that costs $85. What is the mark-up rate based on the selling price?

11. An item that sells for $180 has a mark-up of 40% of the selling price. What is the cost? (Hint: Use the formula:

$$S = \frac{C}{1 - R(s)},$$

where S = selling price, C = the cost, and $R(s)$ = percent of selling price.)

12. In 1988 Sam paid $1,128 in federal income tax. In 1989 he paid $1,456. What was the percent of increase in Sam's income tax from 1988 to 1989?

13. The annual snowfall along the New Hampshire seacoast was 34.5 inches in 1986, and 46 inches in 1987. What was the percent of increase between 1986 and 1987?

14. What is the mark-up on a television selling for $379, if the mark-up rate is 22% of the selling price?

15. A local jeweler sells for $18.04 a travel alarm clock that cost $12.95. What is the percent mark-up (to the nearest whole number) based on the cost?

16. If the selling price of an item is $69.95 based on a mark-up of 28% of the cost, what would be the most a retailer should pay for the item?

17. The ABC Office equipment store paid $229 for an electric typewriter. The store plans to mark up the cost by 40% of the selling price. What is the selling price?

18. What is the mark-up rate of an item that costs $41 and retails at $65?

Answers to Exercise 7.3

1. $12\frac{1}{2}\%$

2. 50%

3. 9.6%

4. 80.4%

5. 7.7%

6. $18,190

7. 7.2%

8. (a) $62.20; (b) $217.70

9. (a) $41.73; (b) 35%

10. 32%

11. $108

12. 29%

13. $33\frac{1}{3}\%$

14. $83.38

15. 39%

16. $54.65

17. $320.60

18. 58.5%

7.4 Percent Decrease (Mark-down)

Whenever we purchase an item on sale we benefit from a percent decrease. Business managers are constantly facing changing numbers, such as variations in expenses, wage changes, or drops in sales.

The amount of decrease is equal to the rate of decrease multiplied by the original amount. Again, use our familiar equation $P = R \times B$ to determine amount of decrease.

Example 1. A new dress, which usually sells at $160, is discounted at 20%. What is the amount of decrease?

$$\begin{aligned} \text{Amount of decrease} &= \text{Rate of decrease} \times \text{Original amount} \\ &= 0.20 \times \$160 \\ &= \$32 \end{aligned}$$

Example 2. Last week the price of gasoline decreased by 5%. If a gallon of gasoline sold for $1.10 before the decrease, what was the amount of decrease?

$$\begin{aligned} P &= R \times B \\ &= 0.05 \times \$1.10 \\ &= \$0.06 \text{ or 6 cents} \end{aligned}$$

Example 3. If the original price was $1.09 and the new price was $1.04, what is the rate of decrease?

First, we must find the amount of decrease.

$$\begin{aligned} \text{Amount of decrease} &= \text{Original price} - \text{New price} \\ &= \$1.09 - \$1.04 \\ &= \$0.05 \end{aligned}$$

Then we find the rate of decrease by applying the percentage formula.

$$\begin{aligned} \text{Rate of decrease} &= \frac{\text{Amount of decrease}}{\text{Original amount}} \\ &= \frac{\$0.05}{\$1.09} \\ &= 0.0458 \\ &= 4.58\% \text{ or 5\% rounded to the nearest whole number} \end{aligned}$$

EXERCISE 7.4

1. Your checking account shows a balance of $736. After writing several checks, your balance is $573.45. What is the percent of decrease in your account?

2. An electric typewriter was sold for $275, at a loss of 6%. What was the cost of the typewriter?

3. After a strenuous weekend playing golf and tennis, Sam's weight dropped from 192 lbs. to 179 lbs. What was the percent of decrease in Sam's weight?

4. The Acme Computer Company recently laid off 15% of its employees. If 1,980 of its former workforce are now unemployed, what is the total number of Acme's present workforce?

5. The dividend for XYZ stock decreased from $13.50 per share to $11.85 per share. What was the rate of decrease?

6. A store owner reduced the price of a slow-selling sweater to $45.95. The original selling price was $69.95. What was the mark-down in dollars?

7. What was the mark-down percentage of net sales if the mark-downs were $2,238 on sales of $23,560?

8. Frank turns the thermostat down to 52°F from 68°F each night before retiring. What is the percent of decrease in the thermostat reading?

9. The local hardware store is having a 20%-off sale. An electric screwdriver is discounted $16. Find (a) the original price and (b) the sale price of the electric screwdriver.

10. In the ABC shoe store's after-Christmas sale, winter boots originally priced at $36 were marked down by 25%. The DEF shoe store originally sold the same boots for $32, then marked them down by 20%. Which store offered the better bargain?

11. What is the original price of a lawnmower which has been discounted 40% to $570?

12 The price of a washing machine was marked down from $279 to $210.40. Find the mark-down percent.

13. A break-even point is the point at which revenue equals cost. A sofa which usually sells for $369.95 is advertised at $25 off the selling price. The cost of the sofa is $231.84 and there is an overhead of 40% of the cost. (a) Find the break-even point for the selling price of the sofa. (b) Does the advertised price result in a profit or a loss? How much?

14. A set of cross-country ski bindings is priced at $55, which includes a mark-up of $14. There is an overhead of $7.70. If the bindings are discounted to $48.50, will the sale result in a profit or a loss? How much?

15. Because of inclement weather, the number of people attending the last three games of the New England Patriots season decreased by 20% from the previous season. If there were an average of 83,750 people at the last three games of last year, how many were in attendance this year?

90

Answers to Exercise 7.7

1. $736 − $573.45 = $162.55, the amount of decrease

$$R = \frac{162.55}{736} = 22\% \text{ or } 0.22$$

2. Cost − 6% of the cost = selling price

$$C − 0.06C = \$275$$
$$0.94C = 275$$
$$C = \$292.55$$

3. Amount of decrease = 192 lb − 179 lb = 13 lb

$$R = \frac{13 \text{ lb}}{192 \text{ lb}} = .0677 = 7\%$$

4. $P = R \times B$

$$1,980 = 0.15 \times B$$

$$\frac{1,980}{0.15} = B$$

$$13,200 − 1980 = 11,220$$
$$11,200 = B$$

5. $13.50 − $11.85 = $1.65

$$R = \frac{P}{B} = \frac{1.65}{13.50} = 0.12 \text{ or } 12\%$$

6. $24

7. 9.50%

8. 23.5%

9. (a) $80; (b) $64

10. DEF shoe store
($25.60 versus $27.00)

11. $950

12. 24.6%

13. (a) Break-even point is $324.58;
(b) profit of $20.37

14. Loss of 20¢

15. 67,000

7.5 Discount

Discount is the difference between the regular price and the sale price. Another way to consider this is that the sale price is the difference between the regular price and the discount. Advertisements frequently state discount as a percent of the product's regular price.

Example 1. The Hampton Hardware store is selling its $32 heating lamp for 15% off the regular price. What is the discount?

$$\text{Discount} = \text{Rate of discount} \times \text{Regular price}$$
$$= 0.15 \times \$32$$
$$= \$4.80$$

Example 2. A clothier is selling a sweater, regularly priced at $60 on sale for $45. (a) What is the discount? (b) What is the discount rate?

(a) $\text{Discount} = \text{Regular price} - \text{Sales price}$
$$= \$60 - \$45$$
$$= \$15$$

(b) $\text{Discount rate} = \dfrac{\text{Discount}}{\text{Regular price}}$
$$= \dfrac{\$15}{\$60}$$
$$= 0.25$$
$$= 25\%$$

Exercise 7.5

1. A snow blower which regularly sells for $600 is on sale for $75 off the regular price. What is the discount rate?

2. The marked price (regular price) of a computer is $1,525. What is the sale price if the rate of discount is 15%?

3. Many companies offer a small discount if you pay your bill promptly. John will get a 3% discount on his $537.38 bill if he pays the bill within 10 days. If John takes advantage of his discount, how much will he pay?

4. During an after-Christmas sale, a local furniture store is selling chairs at $86 less 20%. What is the total price a customer pays for a set of four chairs?

5. A wrist watch is on sale for $95 after a discount (mark-down) of 45% off the regular price. What is the regular price?

Answers to Exercise 7.5

1. $R = \dfrac{\$75}{\$600} = 0.125 = 12.5\%$

2. Discount = $0.15 \times \$1525 = \$228.75$

   Sale price = Marked price − Discount

   $= \$1525 - \$228.75$

   $= \$1296.25$

3. Discount = $0.03 \times \$537.38 = \$16.12$

   Discounted payment = $\$537.38 - \$16.12 = \$521.26$

4. $4 \times \$86 = \$344$

   Discount = $\$344 \times 0.20 = \$68.80$

   Total price = $\$344 - \$68.80 = \$275.20$

5. Discount = Rate of discount × Regular price

   $\$95 = 0.55 \times$ Regular price

   $\dfrac{95}{0.55} =$ Regular price

   $\$172.73 =$ Regular price

7.6 Sales Tax

Most states collect a sales tax on selected products to raise revenue for government expenses and services. The tax rates vary from state to state, as do the types of products being taxed. Not only do states charge a sales tax, but so do cities, towns, and counties. A sales tax is also called a personal property tax. A sales tax is a percentage of the price of an item; that is,

Sales tax = Sales tax rate × Price of an item.

This is another example of our now familiar percentage formula, $P = R \times B$.

Example 1. Mark has just purchased a new car for $11,750. A sales tax of 5% must be paid on his car. How much must he pay?

Sales tax = Sales tax rate × Price of item
= 0.05 × $11,750
= $587.50

Example 2. What is the sales tax rate if the sales tax is $1.26 on an item priced at $42?

$P \quad = R \times B$

$\$1.25 = R \times 42$

$\dfrac{\$1.26}{42} = R$

$0.03 \quad = R = 3\%$

EXERCISE 7.6

1. The price of an item is $120 and the tax rate is 2.5%. What is the amount of sales tax?

2. The total price of an item is equal to the purchase price plus the amount of sales tax. What is the total price of an item selling for $439.50 if the sales tax rate is 3.5%?

3. The purchase price of a sapphire ring is $549. You also have to pay a state sales tax of 6% and a city sales tax of 1.5%. What is the total cost of the ring?

4. Michele has purchased several items totaling $378.10. A sales tax of $4\frac{1}{4}\%$ also must be paid, in addition to a delivery charge of $17.36. What will be the total cost of Michele's purchase?

5. Lorraine bought a new dress with a retail price of $195. The sales tax was $3\frac{1}{2}$%. She paid cash and received a 5% cash discount. What was her total cost?

6. When more than one tax is being levied, the tax rates can be added together to determine the total sales tax. Try problem 3 again this time adding the state sales tax rates together.

7. Determine the sales tax rate if the sales tax is $14.20 on an item which sells for $495.

8. Malcolm bought a new battery for $65.95 and two new tires at $73 each. The sales tax on these items is 6%. What is the total amount of the purchase?

9. Roger has to pay a city tax of $3\frac{1}{2}$% and a county tax of $2\frac{3}{4}$% on his purchase of a new golf cart, which he bought for $850.99. How much tax did he pay?

10. The following items were purchased at the local supermarket: milk, $1.59; eggs, $1.05; shaving cream, $2.78; light bulbs, $4.15; meat, $13.38; aluminum foil, $3.46. If there is a 4% sales tax on nonfood items, what is the total amount of sales tax paid on the above items?

11. Determine the sales tax rate for a garden cart that sells for $250 plus sales tax of $8.75.

12. Eugene purchased an item for $139.00. He paid cash and received a 2.5% discount. The sales tax was 2.25%. What was the total amount of Eugene's payment?

13. Alice purchased three pairs of designer jeans for $41.50 per pair. She had to pay a delivery charge of $11.30 and a sales tax of 3.8% on her purchase. If Alice pays within ten days, she gets an $8\frac{1}{2}$% discount. What is the total cost of the jeans if Alice pays within ten days?

14. Some states charge a meal tax on any meal costing over one dollar. Other states tax on various fractional parts of a dollar as indicated in the table below.

4.5% Sales Tax Rate

Amount	Tax
1 to 9 cents	none
10 to 28 cents	1 cent
29 to 47 cents	2 cents
48 to 68 cents	3 cents
69 to 89 cents	4 cents
90 cents to $1.00	5 cents

Plus 5 cents on each dollar

Using the above table, find the meal tax on the following sales:
(a) 35 cents; (b) $3.15; (c) $57.37

15. A business had a day's receipts of $3,714, which included a 2% sales tax. How much were the sales?

16. What were the sales on receipts of $9,384, which include a 6% sales tax?

17. Determine the sales tax rate on an item costing $63.50 if the sales tax was $2.54.

Answers to Exercise 7.6

1. Sales tax $= 0.025 \times \$120 = \$3$

2. $\$439.50 \times 0.035 = \$15.38$ (sales tax)
   Total price $= \$439.50 + \$15.38 = \$454.88$

3. $\$549 \times 0.06 = \$32.94$ (state sales tax)
   $\$549 \times 0.015 = \$8.24$ (city sales tax)
   $\$549 + \$32.94 + \$8.24 = \$590.18$ (total cost)

4. $\$378.10 \times 0.0425 = \$16.07$ (sales tax)
   $\$378.10 + \$16.07 + \$17.36 = \$411.53$ (total cost)

5. $\$195 \times 0.05 = \$9.75$ (discount)
   $\$195 - \$9.75 = \$185.25$ (sales price)
   $\$185 \times 0.035 = \$6.48$ (sales tax)
   $\$185.25 + \$6.48 = \$191.73$ (total cost)

6. State sales tax + City sales tax = Total sales tax
   $6\% + 1.5\% = 7.5\%$
   $\$549 \times 0.075 = \$41.18$
   $\$549 + \$41.18 = \$590.18$ (total cost)

7. Sales tax rate $= \dfrac{\text{Sales tax}}{\text{Purchase price}} = \dfrac{\$14.20}{\$495} = 0.0286 = 2.9\%$

8. $224.67

9. $53.19

10. 42 cents

11. 3.5%

12. 138.58

13. $129.55

14. (a) 2 cents; (b) 16 cents; (c) $2.87

15. $3,641.18

16. $8,852.83

17. 4%

7.7 Property Tax

Our discussion of property tax will be limited to *real property tax*. Real property tax is paid on land and buildings, whereas personal property tax is paid on such items as clothing and automobiles, as discussed in the previous section.

Property tax is assessed using the formula:
Property tax = Tax rate × Assessed valuation

Does this look familiar? It's another variation of $P = R \times B$.

The assessed valuation is defined to be the rate of assessment multiplied by the fair market value. The tax rate is usually given in one of two ways, as a percent or as a dollar amount per $1,000.

Example 1. The property tax rate in Franklin is $18.75 per $1,000 of assessed value. How much tax must Steve pay if his property is assessed at $87,900?

We must first determine how many $1,000s there are in $87,900.

$$\frac{\$87,900}{\$1,000} = 87.9$$

Next we must multiply 87.9 by the tax rate per $1000.

$$87.9 \times \$18.75 = \$1,648.13$$

This is the amount of the annual property tax Steve must pay.

Example 2. If the property tax rate is 3.25% in the town of Rye, what is the property tax on a house having an assessed valuation of $52,400?

$$\begin{aligned}
\text{Property tax} &= \text{Tax rate} \times \text{Assessed valuation} \\
&= 0.0325 \times \$52,400 \\
&= \$1,703
\end{aligned}$$

EXERCISE 7.7

1. A house has been assessed at $225,000. The property tax rate is 2.95%. Find the property tax.

2. An office condominium building has been assessed at $760,000 in a city whose tax rate is $12.50 per $1,000 of assessed valuation. Find the property tax.

3. The tax rate is defined to be the town's total annual budget divided by the town's total assessed valuation. That is,

$$\text{Property tax rate} = \frac{\text{Total annual budget}}{\text{Total assessed valuation}}.$$

   The total annual budget for the town is $3,475,300, and the total assessed valuation is $49,347,000. What is the property tax rate to the nearest thousandth of a percent?

4. If the assessed value of a house is $34,500 and the tax rate is $16.50 per $1,000, what is the amount of property tax to be paid?

5. Determine the property tax rate given a budget of $721,400 and an assessed value of $3,150,000. Give your answer to the nearest tenth of a percent.

6. How much property tax must be paid on property having an assessed value of $123,200 if the tax rate is 2.04%?

7. Determine the amount of property tax on property whose assessed value is $316,700, at a tax rate of $12.34 per thousand.

8. What is the property tax rate for a town whose total budget is $3,719,304 and whose total assessed value is $79,570,000?

9. In problem 8, what will be the tax rate (a) per $1.00; (b) per $100; (c) per $1,000?

10. The tax rate in New Ulm is $.0515 per $1.00 of assessed valuation. How much tax must the Hansons pay on two pieces of real estate valued at $54,000 and $31,000, if these two pieces are assessed at 65% of their value?

11. The Rices' house and lot are valued at $137,700 in a district where property is assessed at 45% of its fair market value. What amount of property tax will Rice pay if the town's total budget is $3,475,300 and the total assessed valuation is $49,347,000?

12. The property tax on a building is $1,407.45. If the tax rate is 1.36%, find the assessed value, correct to the nearest dollar.

13. Some communities express their tax rate in mills. (1 mill = 0.001 of a dollar). Thus in problem 7, the tax rate of $12.34 per thousand could have been expressed as 12.34 mills, or 13 mills rounded to the nearest whole mill. Change each of the following tax rates to dollars and cents per $100 assessed valuation: (a) 23.7 mills; (b) $0.253; (c) $0.0128.

14. Determine the amount of property tax on property whose value is $244,700, assessed at 71% of its fair market value. The tax rate is 34 mills.

15. The assessed value of a piece of property is $254,000, and the property tax is $3,762. Find the tax rate correct to the nearest whole mill.

16. Determine the amount of property tax on property whose assessed valuation is $19,950 at a tax rate of 23.7 mills per dollar.

100

Answers to Exercise 7.7

1. $P = 0.0295 \times \$225,000 = \$6,637.50$

2. $\dfrac{\$760,000}{1,000} = 760$

   $760 \times \$12.50 = \$9,500$

3. Property tax rate $= \dfrac{\$3,475,300}{\$49,347,000} = 0.070425 = 7.043\%$

4. $\dfrac{\$34,500}{1000} = 34.5$

   $34.5 \times \$16.50 = \$569.25$

5. Property tax rate $= \dfrac{\$721,400}{\$3,150,000} = 0.22901 = 22.9\%$

6. $2,513.28

7. $3,908.08

8. 4.67%

9. (a) $0.0467; (b) $4.67; (c) $46.70

10. $2,845.38

11. $4,337.55

12. $103.489

13. (a) $2.37; (b) $25.30; (c) $1.28

14. $5,907.06

15. 15 mills

16. $472.82

7.8 Simple Interest

If we borrow money from a bank, we pay *interest* for the use of the loan. For example, if the interest rate is 9%, we have to pay back the amount we borrowed plus 9% of the amount. Conversely, when you deposit money into a savings account, the bank will pay you interest for the use of your money. Suppose a bank will you give 5% simple interest on the money you deposit in your account. If you place a sum of money in your account and leave it there for one year, you will then have the original sum plus 5% in your account.

The interest earned on the original sum is called *simple interest*. The interest we earn can be added to the original sum and included in subsequent calculations of interest. The interest calculated in this way is called *compound interest*. In this text we will discuss only simple interest.

Three factors determine the amount of simple interest, whether you borrow money or save money. These three factors are principal, rate of interest, and time. The *principal*, denoted by P, is the amount of money borrowed or saved. The *rate* of interest, denoted by R, is a percent per period of time, usually a year. The *time*, denoted by T, is expressed in years (or a fraction of a year).

The simple interest formula is:
$I = PRT$

Example 1. Find the simple interest earned on a deposit of $1,110 at 6.5% for a period of 1 year.

$I = PRT$
$P = \$1,110$
$R = 6.5\% = 0.065$
$T = 1$
$I = (\$1,110)(0.065)(1)$
$\quad = \$72.15$

Example 2. Find the simple interest owed on $650 borrowed at $4\frac{1}{4}\%$ for 9 months.

In this problem we must convert 9 months to an equivalent part of one year before we use our formula.

$9 \text{ months} = \dfrac{9}{12} \text{ yr} = \dfrac{3}{4} \text{ yr} = 0.75 \text{ yr.}$

$I = PRT$
$\quad = (\$650)(0.0425)(0.75)$
$\quad = \$20.72$

If the time is expressed in days, we must convert it to an equivalent part of one year. There are two ways of doing this. With the *exact method,* the time in years is equal to the number of days divided by 365. With the *ordinary method* (also referred to as the banker's method), the time in years equals the number of days divided by 360. We will use the ordinary method in this text.

Example 3. Find the simple interest owed on $980 at 5.5% for 90 days.

$90 \text{ days} = \dfrac{90}{360} \text{ yr} = \dfrac{1}{4} \text{ yr} = 0.25 \text{ yr.}$

$I = PRT$
$\quad = (\$980)(0.055)(0.25)$
$\quad = \$13.48$

Example 4. The interest on a 45-day loan of $7,600 is $52.25. Find the simple interest rate.

$I = PRT$

Therefore $\dfrac{I}{PT} = R$

That is, $R = \dfrac{I}{PT}$

$\quad = \dfrac{\$52.25}{(\$7600)(\frac{45}{360})}$

$\quad = \dfrac{\$52.25}{(\$7600)(\frac{1}{8})}$

$\quad = \dfrac{\$52.25}{\$950} = 0.055 = 5\frac{1}{2}\%$

Here is a summary of the time conversions.

Time in months: $T = \dfrac{\text{Time in months}}{12}$ yr

Time in days (ordinary method): $T = \dfrac{\text{Time in days}}{360}$ yr

Certain problems involving simple interest require us to calculate the time before we can use $I = PRT$.

Example 5. How much simple interest will be earned on a deposit of $7,000 at 8%, if the money is deposited on July 25 and is withdrawn on September 8?

We must first determine the amount of time; that is, the total number of days.

Number of days in July:	31
Starting July date:	25
Number of July days to be counted (31 − 25):	6
Number of August days to be counted:	31
Number of September days to be counted:	8
Total number of days (6 + 31 + 8):	45

$I = PRT$
$= (\$7,000)(0.08)(\tfrac{45}{360})$
$= (\$7,000)(0.08)(0.125)$
$= \$70$

The *amount* is defined as the sum of the principal and the interest:

To determine the amount, we must first find the interest, then add it to the principal.

Example 6.

$A = P + I$
$= \$780 + \$38.50$
$= \$818.50$

Example 7. Determine the total amount of a loan of $600 at $4\frac{3}{4}$% for half a year.

$$I = PRT$$
$$= (\$600)(0.0475)(\tfrac{1}{2})$$
$$= \$14.25$$

Then find A.

$$A = P + I$$
$$= \$600 + \$14.25$$
$$= \$614.25$$

Example 8. What amount of money will be needed on December 11 to repay a loan taken on September 27 for $4,800 at the simple interest rate of 10.5%? First, we need to determine the number of days.

September days:　3
October days:　31
November days:　30
December days:　$\underline{11}$
　　　　　　　　75

Second, we need to determine the interest.

$$I = PRT$$
$$= (\$4,800)(0.105)(\tfrac{75}{360})$$
$$= \$105$$

Third, we need to determine the amount.

$$A = P + I$$
$$= \$4,800 + \$105$$
$$= \$4,905$$

EXERCISE 7.8

1. Find I if P = $550, R = 8%, and T = 6 months.

2. Determine the yearly rate of interest if $700 is borrowed for 18 months with an interest of 68.25.

3. Find P if R = 12%, I = $336, and T = 42 months.

4. What is the simple interest earned on a 75-day loan of $4,500 at an annual interest rate of 9%?

5. What is the simple interest charged on a loan of $450 at $9\frac{3}{4}$% if the loan is borrowed on May 18 and is to be repaid on August 6?

6. Find I if P = $4,500, R = 5.5%, and T = 2 years.

7. Find R if P = $450, I = $20.25, and T = 6 months.

8. Find P if I = $27, T = 60 days, and R = 7%. (Use 360 days = 1 year.)

9. What is the interest paid on a $4,570 loan for 45 days at 11%?

10. What is the interest paid on a principal of $9,850 at 9.3% from September 19 to November 12? (Use 360 days = 1 year.)

11. What is the simple interest due on a loan of $10,500 borrowed from a bank for 18 months at an annual interest rate of $7\frac{1}{2}$%)

12. The Green Tree Florist purchased a small delivery van for $24,000 and financed the full amount for 3 years at a simple annual interest rate of 12%. Find the monthly payments.

13. After 3 months, Jack repaid a loan of $1,300 plus interest of $21.75. What was the rate of interest on his loan?

14. A local builder wishes to borrow money to build a house on speculation. His local bank loans him $60,000 at 8% simple interest. The loan is due in 90 days. Find the maturity value. Maturity value is the same as amount.
$M = P + I$

15. Recall that $A = P + I$. (Amount equals principal plus interest.) Since $I = PRT$, $A = P + PRT$, or $A = P(1 + RT)$. Using the formula $A = P(1 + RT)$, what investment at 12% simple interest would have a maturity value of $500 in 18 months? (Hint: Solve the formula for P in terms of A, R, and T.)

16. A 90-day note is dated July 10. Find the maturity date of the loan (that is, the date the loan is to be repaid).

17. Find the maturity date of a 6-month note dated August 12, 1900.

18. A loan balance was $5,387.33 one month and $5,014.97 the following month. How much interest was paid if the total payment was $390?

19. How much interest is charged for a month if there is a balance of $450 and the interest rate is 18% a year on the unpaid balance?

Answers to Exercise 7.8

1. $I = PRT = (\$550)(0.08)(\frac{1}{2}) = \$22$

2. $I = PRT$

   $R = \dfrac{I}{RT} = \dfrac{\$68.25}{(\$700)(\frac{18}{12})} = 6.5\%$

3. $I = PRT$

   $P = \dfrac{I}{RT} = \dfrac{\$336}{(0.12)(\frac{42}{12})} = 800$

4. $I = PRT = (\$4,500)(0.09)(\frac{75}{360}) = \$84.38$

5. There are 80 days between the dates.

   $I = (\$450)(0.0975)(\frac{80}{360}) = \$9.75$

6. $495

7. 9%

8. $2,314.29

9. $62.84

10. $137.40

11. $1181.25

12. $906.67

13. 6.7%

14. $61,200

15. $423.73

16. October 8

17. February 12, 1991

18. $17.64

19. $6.75

7.9 Installment Loans

Installment loans are frequently used to finance the cost of items such as furniture, large appliances, and automobiles. Consumers also use credit cards to purchase retail items, thereby having the use of the item before it is fully paid. The consumer then pays for the product in equal installments; this is another type of installment loan. The disadvantage of installment payments to the consumer is that there is an additional expense. Imagine that you wish to buy a TV whose cost is $200. If you give a down payment of $50 and pay nine monthly payments of $20, you will end up paying $230 for the TV.

The *amount* financed is equal to the cash price minus the down payment.

The *finance charge* is equal to the amount financed times the interest rate times the time. In other words, it is $I = PRT$, dressed in new clothing. The rate in $I = PRT$ is called the annual percentage rate.

The *total of the installment payments* is the amount financed plus the finance charge.

The *monthly payment* is equal to the total of the installment payments divided by the number of monthly payments.

Example 1. Mark borrowed $450 from a friend. The money was paid back in 20 monthly payments of $28.20. How much was Mark's finance charge?

20 monthly payments $\times$ $28.20 = $564

$564 − $450 = $114

Example 2. A snow blower is priced at $900 cash or $90 down and 10 monthly payments. The finance charge is $12\frac{1}{2}\%$ of the unpaid balance. Find the amount of each monthly payment.

Unpaid balance: $900 − $90 = $810

Finance charge: $810 $\times$ 0.125 = $101.25

Monthly payment: ($810 + $101.25) $\div$ 10 = $91.13

Occasionally, consumers will pay off a loan early. Should you pay off a loan early, you will be entitled to receive back some of the prepaid interest. The lender will determine the amount of your interest rebate by using a technique known as the *Sum of the Digits method*.

To determine the amount of your rebate of interest using the Sum of the Digits method, you multiply the interest charged by the *rebate fraction*. The rebate fraction has a numerator equal to the sum of the digits of the remaining payments, and a denominator equal to the sum of the digits of the total number of payments.

Example 3. Salim has a 12-month loan which he pays off in 9 months. What is the rebate fraction?

$$\text{Rebate fraction} = \frac{\text{Sum of the digits of the remaining payments}}{\text{Sum of the digits of the total payments}}$$

$$= \frac{1 + 2 + 3}{1 + 2 + 3 + \ldots + 11 + 12}$$

$$= \frac{6}{78}$$

$$= \frac{1}{13}$$

The summing of digits can be cumbersome, especially when there are a large number of digits to be added. Using the summation formula below can save us time.

$\text{Sum} = N\dfrac{(N + 1)}{2}$, where N is the number of payments.

Example 4. Find the rebate fraction for Salim's loan (Example 3) using the summation formula.

The numerator consisted of three remaining payments; thus $N = 3$.

$$\text{Sum of } 1 + 2 + 3 = \frac{3(3 + 1)}{2}$$
$$= 6$$

The denominator consisted of twelve payments; thus $N = 12$.

$$\text{Sum of } 1 + 2 + 3 + \ldots + 12 = \frac{12(12 + 1)}{2}$$
$$= 78$$

So the rebate fraction $= \dfrac{6}{78}$.

Notice that the sum of the digits of the total payments is 78 when there are 12 payments. Since this is often the case, the Sum of the Digits method is also known as the Rule of 78ths. When there are 12 payments, the denominator of the rebate fraction is 78.

Example 5. A 12-month installment loan with $55 payments and an interest charge of $40 was paid in full at the end of 8 months. How much was the final payment?

Step 1: Find the rebate fraction.

Numerator: $\dfrac{4(4 + 1)}{2} = 10$

Denominator: 78   The rebate fraction is $\dfrac{10}{78}$ or $\dfrac{5}{39}$.

Step 2: Find the rebate.

Rebate = rebate fraction × interest charged.
$$= \frac{10}{78} \times \$40$$
$$= \$5.13$$

Step 3: Find the amount still owed.

$55 × 4 payments = $220

Step 4: Find the final payment.

Final payment = amount still owed − interest rebate
$$= \$220 - \$5.13$$
$$= \$214.87$$

EXERCISE 7.9

1. Steve and Elizabeth recently bought new living room furniture on an installment plan of 18 monthly payments of $60 each, with a down payment of $50. If they had paid cash they would have paid $1,000. How much in addition did they pay for buying on the installment plan?

2. Brigitte has just purchased a new stereo system on sale for $1,450. She bought it on the installment plan. She paid a down payment of $250 and financed the unpaid balance over 9 months at 10.5%. What is her monthly payment?

3. A charge of $275 was made August 15 on a credit card. The billing date was September 1; the due date is 30 days after the billing date. If the bill was paid on September 17, find the finance charge.

4. The credit card company in problem 3 charged a monthly finance charge of 1.2% on the unpaid balance. What would the balance on the $275 purchase be on October 2?

5. A car stereo, purchased for $675 with a down payment of $100, is financed at a simple interest rate of $6\frac{3}{4}$% for a period of 9 months. Find the monthly payment.

6. A hospital bill of $735 was paid for with $75 down and $60 a month for 12 months. What was the finance charge?

7. The last month's unpaid balance on Maria's Sears charge was $527.17. (a) If the monthly finance charge is 1.9% of the unpaid balance, what is Maria's finance charge? (b) If Maria made a purchase of $62.30 and also made a payment of $125, what is the total owed?

8. Simple interest is called "add-on" interest. Eugene recently bought a new car costing $12,500 on an installment plan. He made a down payment of 25% and will pay 10.25% simple add-on interest on the unpaid balance for 3 years. What is the amount financed?

9. Determine (a) the total interest paid and (b) the total installment price in problem 8.

10. The Lobster Trap Restaurant accepts VISA and MasterCard. Both VISA and MasterCard have a service charge of 5% on credit card purchases. If the Lobster Trap Restaurant had monthly VISA card sales of $35,700 and monthly MasterCard sales of $18,250, how much was paid (a) to VISA and (b) to MasterCard? The net credit card sales equals the amount remaining after subtracting the service charge. (c) Find the net credit card sales of the Lobster Trap Restaurant.

11. An 8% add-on loan for $4,700 for 30 months was used to purchase a used fishing boat. How much was the interest?

12. Roger has agreed to finance the purchase of a new truck priced at $14,550, minus the trade-in on his car valued at $650, at 16% for four years. His monthly payments will be $474.92. What would the payoff amount be for Roger's truck after he made (a) 24 payments? (b) 36 payments?

13. A loan is being paid in twelve equal monthly payments. At the end of the sixth month the loan is completely paid. What fractional part of the total interest need not be paid?

14. Lisa bought a new pair of skis and ski poles for $1,380. She made a down payment of $200 and agreed to pay the balance over 2 years at 10%. If she was able to pay off her loan in 12 months, how much was the pay-off amount?

Answers to Exercise 7.9

1. $50 + ($60 × 18) = $1,130
   $1,130 − $1,000 = $130

2. $1,450 − $250   = $1,200, the amount financed
   $1,200(0.105)($\frac{9}{12}$) = $94.50, the finance charge
   $1,200 + $94.50 = $1,294.50, the total installment payment
   $1,294.50 ÷ 9   = $143.83, the monthly payment

3. $0

4. $275 × 0.012 = $3.30
   $275 + $3.30 = $278.30

5. $67.12

6. $60.00

7. (a) $10.02; (b) $474.49

8. $9,375

9. (a) $2,882.81; (b) $15,382.81

10. (a) $1,785; (b) $912.50; (c) $51,252.50

11. $940

12. (a) $9,128.53; (b) $5109.24

13. $\frac{21}{78}$

14. $660.84

III

Graphs

Company A			
Company B			
Company C			

5   10   15   20

25%
Marketing

45%
Salaries

20%
Development

10%
Overhead

8.0 BAR GRAPHS

Bar graphs have a horizontal axis and a vertical axis (see figure 8.1). The two axes are labeled with data, enabling you to answer questions by reading the graph. Usually the graph represents approximate numbers rather than exact numbers. Each bar graph has a title, specifying what type of information is being shown.

Figure 8.1
Bar graph

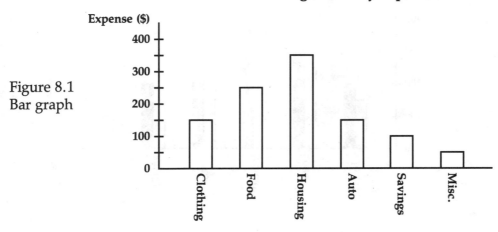

Bar graphs can have vertical bars, as in Figure 8.1, or horizontal bars, as in Figure 8.2.

Figure 8.2
Horizontal
bar graph

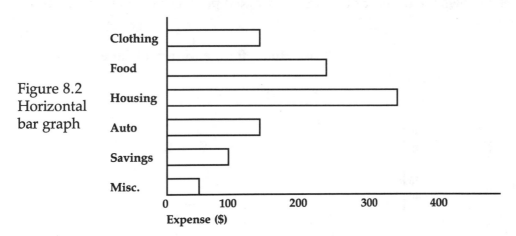

A double bar graph can be used to compare two sets of data. For example, Mark's average monthly expenses for two successive years are compared in Figure 8.3.

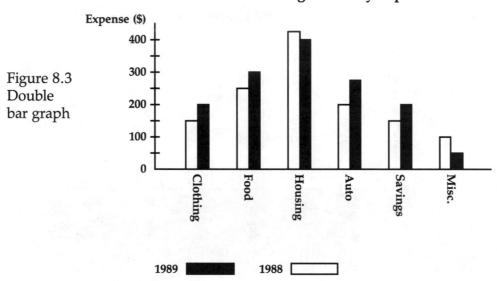

Mark's Average Monthly Expenses

Figure 8.3
Double
bar graph

1989 ■   1988 ☐

Example 1. Lisa works part-time for a mortgage company. The bar graph in Figure 8.4 shows the number of hours she worked per week during the month of June.

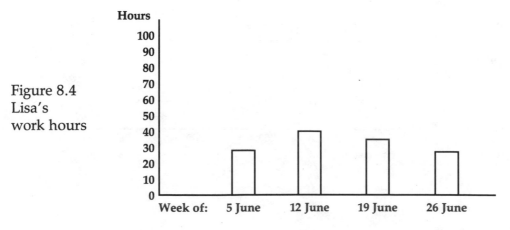

Lisa's Work Hours for the Month of June

Figure 8.4
Lisa's
work hours

(a) How many hours did Lisa work during the week of June 12?
   40 hours

(b) How many hours did Lisa work during the week of June 5?
   28 hours

(c) What was the percent increase of hours worked from the first week of June to the second week?

$$\frac{40 - 28}{28} \times 100$$

$$= 43\%$$

(d) What percent of Lisa's total June hours is represented by the hours worked during the third week of June?

$$\frac{35}{28 + 40 + 35 + 27} \times 100$$

$$= 26.9\% \text{ or } 27\%$$

EXERCISE 8.0

**Pennyroyal Herb Farm
Yearly Profits and Losses**

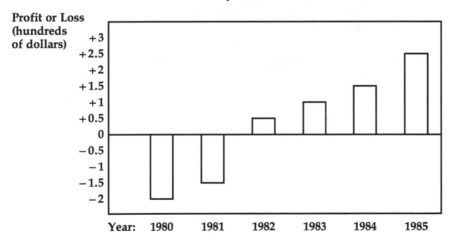

Use the above graph to answer questions 1–5.

1. During which year did the herb farm earn the most money?

2. Which year showed the greatest loss?

3. How much more was earned in 1984 than in 1983?

4. What was the percent increase in profits from 1982 to 1984?

5. Find the difference between the 1985 sales and the 1981 sales.

Use the graph below to answer questions 6–10.

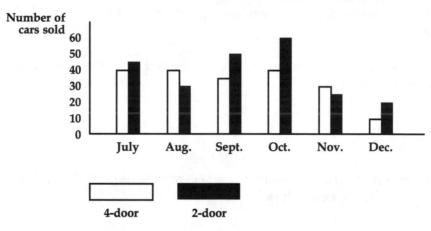

Sales of 4-door Cars versus 2-door Cars

6. How many 4-door cars were sold in September?

7. In which month were the fewest 2-door cars sold?

8. Find the difference between 4-door sales and 2-door sales in August.

9. During which month was there the greatest percent difference in sales between 2-door and 4-door cars?

10. What is the percent difference between 2-door sales and 4-door sales for October?

11. The January through June sales of Troy Clothiers were as follows: Jan., $15,000; Feb., $11,000; March, $12,500; April, $14,000; May, $18,500; June, $16,500. Draw a horizontal bar graph to represent this information.

12. Big Mike's fast food restaurant reported the following sales during the years 1985–1989.

Year	Plain Hamburger	Cheeseburger
1985	$5,000	$6,500
1986	$5,500	$7,500
1987	$6,200	$9,100
1988	$7,300	$10,300
1989	$8,000	$12,500

Construct a double bar graph showing hamburger sales and cheseburger sales.

13. The Beau Brummel Haberdashery listed the following February sales: men's suits, $9,500; men's shoes, $2,700; men's shirts and accessories, $11,000. These were the total sales, including cash sales and credit sales. The cash sales were $7,500 for suits; $1,500 for shoes, and $9,000 for shirts and accessories. Prepare a bar graph showing cash sales, credit sales, and total sales for each of the three departments.

Use the following graph to answer questions 14–18.

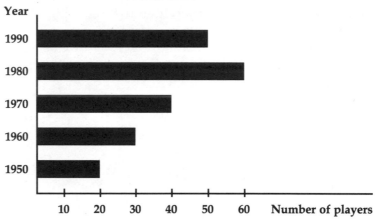

Number of Tennis Players in the Oceanside Tennis Club

14. How many tennis players were there in 1970?

15. Approximately how many more tennis players were there in 1980 than in 1960?

16. Write a ratio comparing the number of tennis players in 1950 to the number in 1990.

17. In what 10-year period did the club membership increase the most?

18. Based on the graph, would you expect an increase or decrease in club membership by the year 2000?

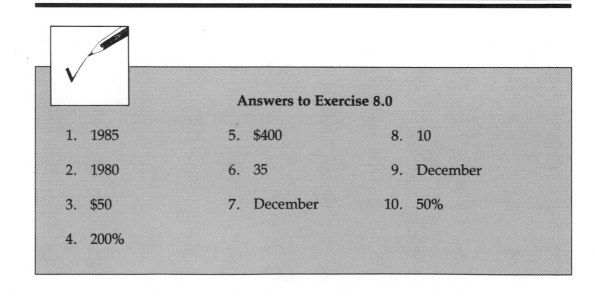

Answers to Exercise 8.0

1. 1985	5. $400	8. 10
2. 1980	6. 35	9. December
3. $50	7. December	10. 50%
4. 200%		

11.

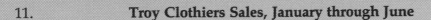

Troy Clothiers Sales, January through June

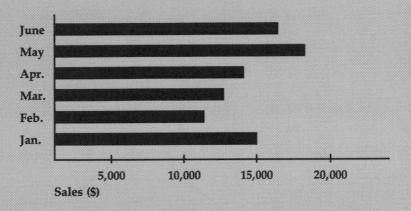

12.

Big Mike's Sales, 1985–1989

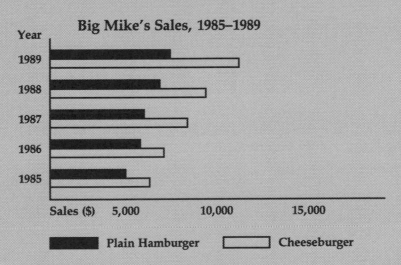

13.

Beau Brummell Haberdashery, February Sales

14. 40   15. 30   16. $\frac{20}{50}$ or $\frac{2}{5}$ 17. Between 1970 and 1980   18. An increase

9.0 LINE GRAPHS

Line graphs are similar to bar graphs, but only the tops of the bars are marked. These points are then joined with a line. See Figure 9.1.

Mark's Average Monthly Expenses

**Figure 9.1
Line graph**

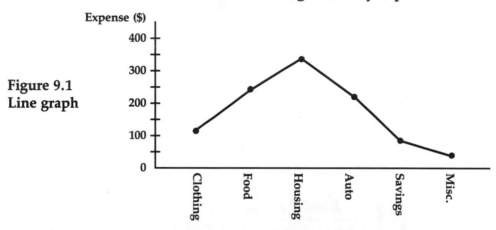

Example 1. The Arc College Publishing Company had monthly profits as shown in the line graph in Figure 9.2.

Arc College Publishing Co. Profit for 1990

**Figure 9.2
Arc Co.
profits**

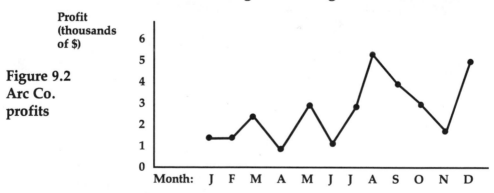

(a) Which month had the greatest profit?
August

(b) Find the company's profit for October.
$3,000

(c) During which month was the company's profit the lowest?
April

(d) Find the company's profit for August.
$5,500

EXERCISE 9.0

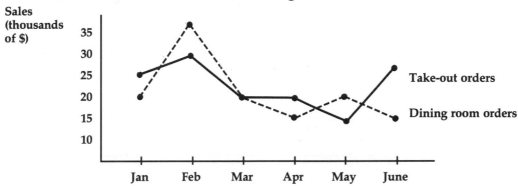

Wok Chinese Restaurant
Sales of Take-out Orders and Dining Room Orders

Use the above graph to answer questions 1–6.

1. Which type of order showed a decline in sales from April to May?

2. What were the total sales for January?

3. By how much did sales of take-out orders decrease between February and March?

4. During which month were the sales of each type of order the same?

5. How much less were the sales of take-out orders than the sales of dining room orders during May?

6. What type of order seemed to be more popular during February?

7. Draw a line graph to represent the sales of Troy Clothiers for the period January through June. Jan., $15,000; Feb., $11,000; March $12,500; April, $14,000; May, $18,500; June, $16,500. (Compare this graph with the bar graph you drew for problem 11 of Exercise 8.1.)

8. Listed below are the sales of the Gerould Publishing Company for the last six months of the year. Prepare a line graph that shows the sales for each month. Use vertical intervals of $25,000.

July	$150,000
August	90,000
September	120,000
October	180,000
November	210,000
December	75,000

Answers to Exercise 9.0

1. Take-out orders

2. $45,000

3. $10,000

4. March

5. $5,000

6. Dining room orders

7.

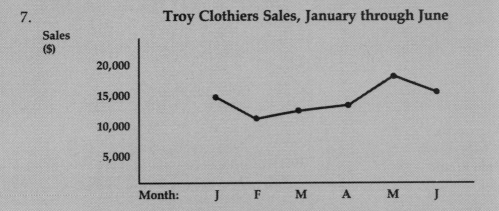

Troy Clothiers Sales, January through June

8.

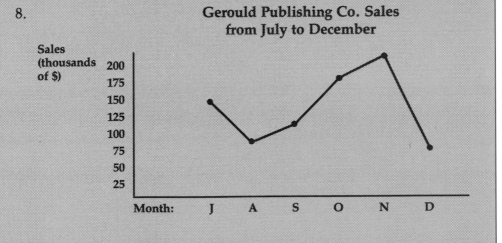

**Gerould Publishing Co. Sales
from July to December**

10.0 CIRCLE GRAPHS

You may recall from high school geometry that a circle contains 360°. When we construct a circle graph, we represent percentages by sectors of a circle (see Figure 10.1). If Mark spends 15% of his income on clothing, then the "Clothing" sector of the circle contains
$360° \times 0.15 = 54°$

Similarly, if Mark spends 26% of his income on food, then the "Food" sector of the circle contains
$360° \times 0.26 = 94°$

A circle graph is also known as a pie graph, because the sectors look like slices of a pie.

Mark's Average Monthly Expenses

**Figure 10.1
Circle graph
(pie graph)**

A personal computer is an excellent tool for constructing circle graphs. If you do not have access to a PC, you will need a compass, a ruler, and a protractor to construct circle graphs.

Example 1. The Holmes Real Estate Company has an annual budget of $275,000. The circle graph in Figure 10.2 shows the percentage of the budget that is allocated to each item.

**Figure 10.2
Holmes Co.
budget**

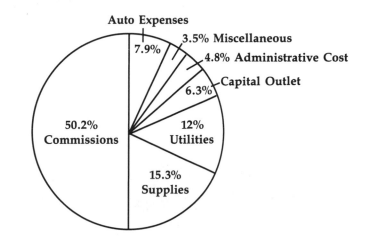

Holmes Real Estate Co. Budget of $275,500

(a) How much money is budgeted for utilities?
    12% of $275,000 = $33,000

(b) How much money is budgeted for auto expenses?
    7.9% of $275,000 = $21,725.00

(c) What percent of the money is budgeted for supplies and utilities?
    15.3% + 12% = 27.3%

(d) What percent of the money is budgeted for commissions and administrative costs?
    50.2% + 4.8% = 55.0%

EXERCISE 10.0

Pennyroyal Herb Farms Advertising Budget

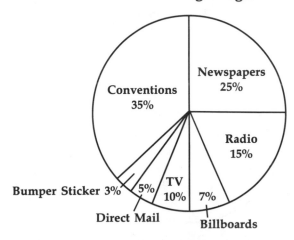

The Pennyroyal Herb Farms Advertising Budget for 1989 was $120,000. Use the circle graph above to answer questions 1–3.

1. What is the dollar amount budgeted for billboards?

2. How much was budgeted for newpapers and radio?

3. What does the budget of $120,000 represent in terms of percent?

4. The revenues of the Pennyroyal Herb Farm were distributed as follows: herbal wreaths, 13%; garden statuary, 24%; fresh cut herbs, 27%; small plants, 36%. Draw a circle graph to represent this information.

5. Prepare a circle graph to illustrate the percentage of A, B, and C students at New Paul College.

A students	4,000
B students	5,600
C students	6,400

Answers to Exercise 10.0

1. $8,400

2. $48,000

3. 100%

4.

Pennyroyal Herb Farm Revenues

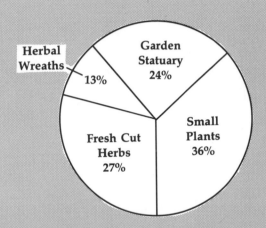

Herbal Wreaths 13%

Garden Statuary 24%

Small Plants 36%

Fresh Cut Herbs 27%

5.

New Paul College: A, B, and C Students

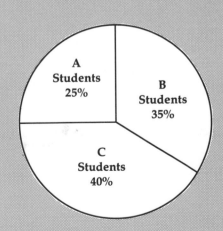

A Students 25%

B Students 35%

C Students 40%

POST TEST

The following test is designed to help you assess your understanding of the basics, applications, and graphs presented in this book. There is no time limit in taking the post test. Answers to the test questions are given at the end of the test. There is a table at the end of the answer key to help you determine your grade.

1. Indicate the place value of each digit in 7,903.

2. Write the number 16,123 in words.

3. 55 + 33 + 16 + 12 = ?

4. Find the sum:
   16,302
   1,711
   548
   13
   7,502

5. If a minuend is 4,781 and the subtrahend is 439, what is the difference?

6. The balance in Samantha's checkbook is $933. If she writes a check for $13.42 and another check for $119.37, what is her new balance?

7. 47,301 − 29,487 = ?

8. 1,836 × 47 = ?

9. Joey bought 9 tickets in a church raffle and paid $4.00 per ticket. How much did she pay?

10. If a case of motor oil contains 32 cans, how many cans of oil would there be in 159 cases?

11. $29,533 \div 7 = ?$

12. What is the average height in inches of 5 children whose heights are: 42 inches, 54 inches, 47 inches, 39 inches, and 53 inches?

(Average height $= \dfrac{\text{Sum of heights}}{\text{Number of children}}$)

13. How much is your weekly pay if your yearly salary is $40,872)

14. Write $\dfrac{16}{46}$ in lowest terms.

15. Convert $5\dfrac{7}{9}$ to an improper fraction.

16. Convert the improper fraction $\dfrac{41}{3}$ to a mixed number.

17. What is the sum of $\dfrac{11}{31} + \dfrac{15}{31} + \dfrac{2}{31} = ?$

18. $\dfrac{3}{5} + \dfrac{2}{7} + \dfrac{1}{3} = ?$

19. $\dfrac{11}{13} - \dfrac{2}{3} = ?$

20. $8\dfrac{1}{6} - 2\dfrac{3}{4} = ?$

21. $14 - (1\dfrac{7}{8} + 3\dfrac{1}{4}) = ?$

22. $\dfrac{4}{9} \times \dfrac{1}{12} = ?$

23. $2\dfrac{2}{3} \times 6\dfrac{3}{5} = ?$

24. $\dfrac{3}{5} \div \dfrac{12}{25} = ?$

25. $22 - 3\dfrac{1}{3} = ?$

26. Write the number 17.23 in words.

27. Convert 0.102 to an equivalent common fraction in lowest terms.

28. Convert $\frac{5}{12}$ to its decimal equivalent, correct to the nearest ten-thousandth.

29. $3.15 + $21.03 + $7.99 = ?

30. The temperature at 1 p.m. was 87.3°. At 8 p.m. it was 64.5°. What was the drop in temperature?

31. If you bought 17 hammers at $7.35 each, how much money did you pay?

32. If you drove 872.7 miles on 19.8 gallons of gasoline, how many miles did you get per gallon of gasoline?

33. Convert 0.637 to a percent.

34. Convert 31.01% to a decimal.

35. Convert $\frac{9}{5}$ to a percent.

36. Convert 30.1% to a fraction.

37. Solve for x: $3x + 7 = 22$

38. Solve for y: $y + 1 = 3y - 5$

39. Solve for z: $2.3 = 0.4z - 21.1$

40. Solve for x: $4x = 2x + ab$

41. Solve for x: $\dfrac{a - b}{x} = 5a$

42. Given $I = PRT$. Find T if $P = $9,000$, $R = 4.5\%$ and $I = 810.

43. Given $A = P(1 + RT)$. Find R if $P = $14,600$, $T = 6$ months and $A = $15,745$.

44. What percent of 300 is 18?

45. 20 is 25% of what number?

46. What is $2\frac{1}{4}\%$ of 430?

47. If you receive a commission of 4.7% of net sales and your net sales totaled $7,532.54, what was your commission?

48. John sold products totaling $12,750 and received a commission of $669.38. What was his rate of commission?

49. What is the mark-up of a table saw that costs $450 and sells for $589.99? What is the rate of mark-up?

50. Each winter morning I turn my thermostat up from 60°F to 68°F. What is the percent increase in the thermostat reading?

51. If the original price of a snow blower has been discounted 35% to $610, what is the original price?

52. A retail store allows its employees a 12% discount on any purchase. How much would an employee pay on an item that normally cost $79.95?

53. A meal at the Gourmet Restaurant cost $34.87. If you had to pay a meal tax of $2\frac{1}{2}$% and you intended to leave a 20% tip, how much would you pay in total?

54. Determine the amount of property tax on property whose assessed value is $237,800 at a tax rate of $11.40 per $1,000.

55. What is the assessed value correct to the nearest dollar on a building if the property tax is $1,407.45 and the tax rate is 1.36%?

56. What is the amount of simple interest paid on a $6,540 loan for 3 months at 12%?

57. What would be the monthly payments in problem 56?

58. A 12-month installment loan with $35 payments and an interest charge of $50 was paid in full at the end of 9 months. How much was the final payment? (Hint: Recall the Rule of 78ths).

59. The manufacturing costs in producing a widget are as follows: Research and development, $136,800; labor, $125,000; material costs, $180,500. Construct a circle graph showing this data.

Use the following graph to answer questions 60–63.

Contributions to the Animal Arts Fund

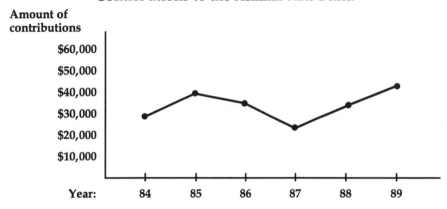

60. In which year were the fewest contributions made?

61. Between what years was the greatest decrease in contributions?

62. What was the average yearly contribution during the five-year period?

63. Write a ratio comparing the contributions in 1986 to those in 1984.

Post Test Answers

1. 7 9 0 3
   Thousands Hundreds Tens Ones

2. Sixteen thousand, one hundred twenty-three

3. 116

4. 26,076

5. 4342 is the difference

6. $800.21

7. 17,814

8. 86,292

9. $36

10. 5,088 cans

11. 4,219

12. 47 inches

13. $786

14. $\frac{8}{23}$

15. $\frac{52}{9}$

16. $13\frac{2}{3}$

17. $\frac{28}{31}$

18. $\frac{128}{105}$ or $1\frac{23}{105}$

19. $\frac{7}{39}$

20. $\frac{65}{12}$ or $5\frac{5}{12}$

21. $\frac{71}{8}$ or $8\frac{7}{8}$

22. $\frac{1}{27}$

23. $\frac{88}{5}$ or $17\frac{3}{5}$

24. $\frac{5}{4}$

25. $\frac{143}{20}$ or $7\frac{3}{20}$

26. Seventeen and twenty-three hundredths

27. $\frac{51}{500}$

28. 0.4167

29. $32.17

30. 22.8

31. $124.95

32. Approximately 44.1 miles per gallon

33. 63.7%

34. 0.3101

35. 180%

36. $\frac{301}{1,000}$

37. $x = 5$

38. $y = 3$

39. $z = 58.5$

40. $x = \frac{ab}{z}$

41. $x = \frac{a-b}{5a}$

42. $T = 2$

43. 15.7%

44. 6%

45. 80

46. 9.675

47. $354.03

48. $5\frac{1}{4}\%$

49. $139.99; 31.1%

50. 13.3%

51. $938.46

52. $70.36

53. $42.71

54. $2,710.92

55. $103,489

56. $196.20

57. $2,245.40

58. $101.15

59.

Manufacturing Costs

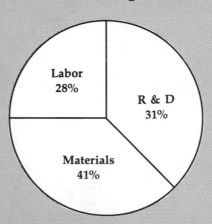

Labor 28%

R & D 31%

Materials 41%

60. 1987

61. Between 1986 and 1987

62. $37,000

63. $\frac{358}{30}$ or $\frac{7}{6}$

Use the table below to determine your letter grade.

Number of Correct Answers	Letter Grade
60–63	A
58–59	A–
56–57	B+
54–55	B
52–53	B–
50–51	C+
48–49	C
46–47	C–
44–45	D+
42–43	D
40–41	D–
39 and under	Work through the book again.

NOTES

THE FIFTY-MINUTE SERIES

Quantity	Title	Code #	Price	Amount
	MANAGEMENT TRAINING			
	Self-Managing Teams	000-0	$7.95	
	Delegating For Results	008-6	$7.95	
	Successful Negotiation — Revised	09-2	$7.95	
	Increasing Employee Productivity	010-8	$7.95	
	Personal Performance Contracts — Revised	12-2	$7.95	
	Team Building — Revised	16-5	$7.95	
	Effective Meeting Skills	33-5	$7.95	
	An Honest Day's Work: Motivating Employees To Excel	39-4	$7.95	
	Managing Disagreement Constructively	41-6	$7.95	
	Training Managers To Train	43-2	$7.95	
	Learning To Lead	043-4	$7.95	
	The Fifty-Minute Supervisor — Revised	58-0	$7.95	
	Leadership Skills For Women	62-9	$7.95	
	Systematic Problem Solving & Decision Making	63-7	$7.95	
	Coaching & Counseling	68-8	$7.95	
	Ethics In Business	69-6	$7.95	
	Understanding Organizational Change	71-8	$7.95	
	Project Management	75-0	$7.95	
	Risk Taking	76-9	$7.95	
	Managing Organizational Change	80-7	$7.95	
	Working Together In A Multi-Cultural Organization	85-8	$7.95	
	Selecting And Working With Consultants	87-4	$7.95	
	PERSONNEL MANAGEMENT			
	Your First Thirty Days: A Professional Image in a New Job	003-5	$7.95	
	Office Management: A Guide To Productivity	005-1	$7.95	
	Men and Women: Partners at Work	009-4	$7.95	
	Effective Performance Appraisals — Revised	11-4	$7.95	
	Quality Interviewing — Revised	13-0	$7.95	
	Personal Counseling	14-9	$7.95	
	Attacking Absenteeism	042-6	$7.95	
	New Employee Orientation	46-7	$7.95	
	Professional Excellence For Secretaries	52-1	$7.95	
	Guide To Affirmative Action	54-8	$7.95	
	Writing A Human Resources Manual	70-X	$7.95	
	Winning at Human Relations	86-6	$7.95	
	WELLNESS			
	Mental Fitness	15-7	$7.95	
	Wellness in the Workplace	020-5	$7.95	
	Personal Wellness	021-3	$7.95	

THE FIFTY-MINUTE SERIES (Continued)

Quantity	Title	Code #	Price	Amount
	WELLNESS (CONTINUED)			
	Preventing Job Burnout	23-8	$7.95	
	Job Performance and Chemical Dependency	27-0	$7.95	
	Overcoming Anxiety	029-9	$7.95	
	Productivity at the Workstation	041-8	$7.95	
	COMMUNICATIONS			
	Technical Writing In The Corporate World	004-3	$7.95	
	Giving and Receiving Criticism	023-X	$7.95	
	Effective Presentation Skills	24-6	$7.95	
	Better Business Writing—Revised	25-4	$7.95	
	Business Etiquette And Professionalism	032-9	$7.95	
	The Business Of Listening	34-3	$7.95	
	Writing Fitness	35-1	$7.95	
	The Art Of Communicating	45-9	$7.95	
	Technical Presentation Skills	55-6	$7.95	
	Making Humor Work	61-0	$7.95	
	Visual Aids In Business	77-7	$7.95	
	Speed-Reading In Business	78-5	$7.95	
	Publicity Power	82-3	$7.95	
	Influencing Others	84-X	$7.95	
	SELF-MANAGEMENT			
	Attitude: Your Most Priceless Possession-Revised	011-6	$7.95	
	Personal Time Management	22-X	$7.95	
	Successful Self-Management	26-2	$7.95	
	Balancing Home And Career—Revised	035-3	$7.95	
	Developing Positive Assertiveness	38-6	$7.95	
	The Telephone And Time Management	53-X	$7.95	
	Memory Skills In Business	56-4	$7.95	
	Developing Self-Esteem	66-1	$7.95	
	Creativity In Business	67-X	$7.95	
	Managing Personal Change	74-2	$7.95	
	Stop Procrastinating: Get To Work!	88-2	$7.95	
	CUSTOMER SERVICE/SALES TRAINING			
	Sales Training Basics—Revised	02-5	$7.95	
	Restaurant Server's Guide—Revised	08-4	$7.95	
	Telephone Courtesy And Customer Service	18-1	$7.95	
	Effective Sales Management	031-0	$7.95	
	Professional Selling	42-4	$7.95	
	Customer Satisfaction	57-2	$7.95	
	Telemarketing Basics	60-2	$7.95	
	Calming Upset Customers	65-3	$7.95	
	Quality At Work	72-6	$7.95	
	Managing Quality Customer Service	83-1	$7.95	
	Quality Customer Service—Revised	95-5	$7.95	
	SMALL BUSINESS AND FINANCIAL PLANNING			
	Understanding Financial Statements	022-1	$7.95	
	Marketing Your Consulting Or Professional Services	40-8	$7.95	

THE FIFTY-MINUTE SERIES (Continued)

Quantity	Title	Code #	Price	Amount
	SMALL BUSINESS AND FINANCIAL PLANNING (CONTINUED)			
	Starting Your New Business	44-0	$7.95	
	Personal Financial Fitness—Revised	89-0	$7.95	
	Financial Planning With Employee Benefits	90-4	$7.95	
	BASIC LEARNING SKILLS			
	Returning To Learning: Getting Your G.E.D.	002-7	$7.95	
	Study Skills Strategies—Revised	05-X	$7.95	
	The College Experience	007-8	$7.95	
	Basic Business Math	024-8	$7.95	
	Becoming An Effective Tutor	028-0	$7.95	
	CAREER PLANNING			
	Career Discovery	07-6	$7.95	
	Effective Networking	030-2	$7.95	
	Preparing for Your Interview	033-7	$7.95	
	Plan B: Protecting Your Career	48-3	$7.95	
	I Got the Job!	59-9	$7.95	
	RETIREMENT			
	Personal Financial Fitness—Revised	89-0	$7.95	
	Financial Planning With Employee Benefits	90-4	$7.95	

OTHER CRISP INC. BOOKS

Quantity	Title	Code #	Price	Amount
	Desktop Publishing	001-9	$ 7.95	
	Stepping Up To Supervisor	11-8	$13.95	
	The Unfinished Business Of Living: Helping Aging Parents	19-X	$12.95	
	Managing Performance	23-7	$19.95	
	Be True To Your Future: A Guide To Life Planning	47-5	$13.95	
	Up Your Productivity	49-1	$10.95	
	Comfort Zones: Planning Your Future 2/e	73-4	$13.95	
	Copyediting 2/e	94-7	$18.95	
	Recharge Your Career	027-2	$12.95	
	Practical Time Management	275-4	$13.95	

VIDEO TITLE*

Quantity	Video Title*	Code #	Preview	Purchase	Amount
	Attitude: Your Most Priceless Possession	012-4	$25.00	$395.00	·
	Quality Customer Service	013-2	$25.00	$395.00	
	Team Building	014-2	$25.00	$395.00	
	Job Performance & Chemical Dependency	015-9	$25.00	$395.00	
	Better Business Writing	016-7	$25.00	$395.00	
	Comfort Zones	025-6	$25.00	$395.00	
	Creativity in Business	036-1	$25.00	$395.00	
	Motivating at Work	037-X	$25.00	$395.00	
	Calming Upset Customers	040-X	$25.00	$395.00	
	Balancing Home and Career	048-5	$25.00	$395.00	
	Stress and Mental Fitness	049-3	$25.00	$395.00	

(*Note: All tapes are VHS format. Video package includes five books and a Leader's Guide.)

THE FIFTY-MINUTE SERIES
(Continued)

	Amount
Total Books	
Less Discount (5 or more different books 20% sampler)	
Total Videos	
Less Discount (purchase of 3 or more videos earn 20%)	
Shipping ($3.50 per video, $.50 per book)	
California Tax (California residents add 7%)	
TOTAL	

☐ Send volume discount information.

☐ Please send me a catalog.

☐ Mastercard ☐ VISA ☐ AMEX

Exp. Date _____

Account No. _____ Name (as appears on card) _____

Ship to: _____ Bill to: _____

_____ _____

_____ _____

_____ _____

Phone number: _____ P.O. # _____

All orders except those with a P.O.# must be prepaid.
For more information Call (415) 949-4888 or FAX (415) 949-1610.